SUPERPOWER RIVALRY:

The Cold War 1945–1991

Tony McAleavy

Humanities Inspector
for Gloucestershire

CAMBRIDGE
UNIVERSITY PRESS

PUBLISHED BY THE PRESS SYNDICATE OF THE UNIVERSITY OF CAMBRIDGE
The Pitt Building, Trumpington Street, Cambridge CB2 1RP, United Kingdom

CAMBRIDGE UNIVERSITY PRESS
The Pitt Building, Trumpington Street, Cambridge CB2 1RP, United Kingdom
40 West 20th Street, New York, NY 10011-4211, USA
10 Stamford Road, Oakleigh, Melbourne 3166, Australia

First published 1998

Printed in the United Kingdom at the University Press, Cambridge

Typeset in Monotype Octavian and FF Meta

A catalogue record for this book is available from the British Library

ISBN 0 521 59739 0 paperback

Produced by Gecko Limited, Bicester, Oxon

Illustrations by Gecko Limited and Gerry Ball

Picture research by Marilyn Rawlings

Acknowledgements
4l and r, 8, 11, 22, 24r, 27, 33, 43, 47 Peter Newark's Historical Pictures; 5, 9
ET Archive; 7, 12, 19, 41, 50 (inset), 50–1, 51 (inset), 57, 58–9, 75, 77 (inset)
Popperfoto; 16, 56, 62, 76–7 AKG London; 17, 20, 40t David King Collection;
21, 24l, 30–1 (and inset) Hulton Getty; 23, 28, 35, 39, 49, 53, 55, 61, 63, 64, 65,
66, 70, 73 Camera Press; 34, 48 Bilderdienst Süddeutscher Verlag; 38, 40b, 46,
52, 67, 71, 74 Topham Picturepoint; 44 Black Star (photo Gordon Cranbourne).

The cover picture shows a Soviet anti-US poster from the Cold War era
(David King).

Contents

The roots of the Cold War

Almost as soon as the Second World War ended, the winners started to argue with each other. In particular, a bitter conflict developed between the USA and the USSR. This struggle continued until the late 1980s. Walter Lippmann, an American journalist writing in the 1940s, called it a 'cold war' and the phrase has been widely used since.

Historians have produced three conflicting explanations for the start of the Cold War:

1   The USSR was to blame. Stalin planned for a communist take-over of the world. The take-over of Eastern Europe was the first step towards world control.

2   The USA was to blame. Soviet actions were defensive. The USA wanted to control its area of influence but refused to allow the USSR to do the same.

3   Neither side was to blame. The Cold War was based on misunderstanding and forces beyond the control of both sides.

Focus

As you find out more about the Cold War, try to work out which of these three explanations you find most convincing.

The long-term causes of the Cold War

The roots of the Cold War are to be found in earlier history. One historian said that the Cold War started, not in the 1940s, but in 1917, when the Russian Revolution took place and Soviet communism was born. By 1917 the USA was the richest country in the world. The two countries were both enormous and both had great natural resources. However, there was no chance of real friendship between them because the leaders of the new Soviet Union had extremely different beliefs from those of American politicians.

AMERICAN CAPITALISM

1   People should be free to make as much money as they can.

2   Factories and other property should be owned by individuals and companies.

3   The government should interfere as little as possible in the lives of ordinary people.

4   At elections people should be allowed to choose anyone they want for the government.

5   The Press should be able to criticise the government.

6   The government should not interfere in religion.

SOVIET COMMUNISM

1   Rich people are wicked and selfish. They should be forced to share their wealth.

2   Factories and other property should be owned by the state on behalf of all the people.

3   A communist government should get involved in every aspect of life.

4   At elections people should only be allowed to choose communists for the government.

5   The Press should never criticise a communist government.

6   Religious belief is nonsense and should be wiped out by the government.

Not only did American and Soviet leaders disagree totally. Each side was completely convinced that it was right and that other countries around the world should follow their lead. Americans believed that the answer to world problems was for other people to learn to live in an American way. The Soviet leaders were sure that their communist ideas would eventually spread to every country in the world. As a result the USA and the Soviet Union were very hostile towards each other after 1917. In 1919 the USA joined Britain, France and other countries in an attempt to destroy Soviet communism by force. They invaded the Soviet Union in support of the White Russians who were engaged in a civil war with the Bolshevik revolutionaries. This use of force failed but the hostility remained.

A female Soviet soldier meets American troops near the River Elbe, 1945. The smiles soon disappeared as the wartime allies became Cold War enemies.

The common enemy

The hostility between the the USA and the Soviet Union was suspended in 1941. They were linked by their common wish to destroy Hitler. As soon as it looked as though Hitler was going to be defeated the old tension began to re-emerge. Hitler predicted that once the war was over the two wartime allies would no longer have anything in common and would become hostile towards each other once again. The end of the war produced a difficult situation. Nazi power over Europe had been destroyed but what should replace it? In many countries there was no proper government. Decisions had to be made about the future of these countries. Inevitably, American and Soviet leaders had very different views on the best type of government for the countries of the new Europe. Shortly before his death, Hitler predicted the start of the Cold War.

'After the collapse of the German Reich, and until there is a rise in nationalism in Asia, Africa or Latin America, there will only be two powers in the world: The United States and Soviet Russia. Through the laws of history and geographical position these giants are destined to struggle with each other either through war, or through rivalry in economics and political ideas.'
Hitler's Political Testament, April 1945

Discussion points

> Explain in your own words the difference between American and Soviet ideas.

> Why did the destruction of Germany make a conflict likely between the USA and the USSR?

1945: the breakdown of the wartime alliance

The victory over Hitler created new worries for the winners. They had different views as to the future of Europe after the war. Before the end of 1945 deep divisions were emerging between the leaders of the USA and the Soviet Union.

Why did the wartime alliance fall apart in 1945?

Yalta and the argument over Poland

In February 1945 the leaders of Britain, the USA and the Soviet Union met at a place called Yalta. The three leaders were Churchill, Roosevelt and Stalin. The end of the war was in sight and they met to decide on the shape of the post-war world. Much of their time was spent discussing the future of Poland. They disagreed about how Poland should be governed.

> ### YALTA: THE ATTITUDES OF THE LEADERS
>
> > Roosevelt was already very ill – two months later he would be dead. Roosevelt was keen that democracy should be introduced into Eastern Europe. However, he trusted Stalin and wanted to make sure that the USA and the USSR remained on good terms after the war.
>
> > Churchill was very concerned about the future of Poland and Eastern Europe. He did not trust Stalin. He wanted to stop Stalin from imposing communism on the territory taken by the Red Army. Britain had gone to war in 1939 to help Poland and Churchill did not want to abandon Poland to Soviet control.
>
> > Stalin was obsessed with the security of the USSR. He wanted the Soviet Union to retain the Polish territory he had taken in 1939 as part of the Nazi–Soviet Pact. He also wanted to make sure that the new government of Poland would be friendly towards the Soviet Union.

Why was Poland the centre of attention at Yalta?

Poland was the largest country in Eastern Europe. Its post-war settlement was likely to set a pattern for the rest of Eastern Europe but the wartime allies had disagreed strongly about that settlement before Yalta.

Two different groups wanted to form the new government for Poland. Each group had a very different relationship with Stalin:

The London Poles

When the war broke out, some members of the Polish government fled to London and set up a 'government-in-exile'. They were strongly anti-Soviet. Much of Poland had been in the Russian Empire before 1917. The London Poles were Catholics and many were landowners: they hated both the idea of communism and Stalin because he had carved up their country through the German–Soviet Pact in 1939. In 1943 they were horrified to learn that the Soviet army had executed about 15,000 Polish officers and buried their bodies at a place called Katyn. Stalin knew that if the London Poles formed a Polish government, it would be hostile to the USSR.

The Lublin Poles

In July 1944 the USSR set up its own future government for Poland. This first met at the town of Lublin, and they became known as the Lublin Poles. They were mostly communists and Stalin felt that they could be trusted.

The Warsaw Uprising

The London Poles decided that their only chance of frustrating Stalin was to seize control of part of Poland before the Red Army did. In August 1944 Polish resistance fighters, loyal to the London Poles, attacked the German forces occupying Warsaw, the capital of Poland. The Soviet army was nearby but did nothing to help the Poles. Stalin did not want them to defeat the Germans. He wanted the Lublin Poles to take over after the war. The British and the Americans were appalled by the Soviet attitude. Without Soviet help, the Rising was ruthlessly smashed by the Germans and nearly 300,000 Poles were killed. The Germans sent the surviving people of Warsaw to concentration camps and when the Red Army finally took the city it was completely deserted. The Red Army went on to take control of the whole of Poland. By January 1945 the USSR announced that Poland had been liberated and the Lublin group was now in charge of Poland.

>> **Activity**

1. Explain in your own words the different attitudes of the leaders who met at Yalta towards Poland.

2. Who were the Lublin Poles and the London Poles?

3. What was the Warsaw Uprising?

4. Why do you think that Stalin refused to help the Warsaw rebels?

SOURCE A

German troops patrol the devastated streets of Warsaw after the abortive uprising.
> Why did Stalin fail to help the Warsaw Rising?

The meeting at Yalta

The three leaders had met before — at the Tehran summit in late 1943. The meeting at Yalta, in the Soviet Union, took place between 4 and 11 February 1945. Stalin had refused to leave the USSR so the two Western leaders had to go to him. The three men were pleased at the way the war was going. President Roosevelt talked about the friendly, 'family' atmosphere of the meeting but beneath the surface, serious disagreements existed.

The discussions at Yalta were very wide-ranging but the future of Poland dominated. The three leaders had previously agreed that the Soviet Union would take land from Poland and Poland would, in turn, be given German land. At Yalta they argued about the details and Churchill tried to limit the changes. He was worried about taking too much land from Germany and said: 'I do not want to stuff the Polish goose until it dies of German indigestion'. There was even greater disagreement about who should govern Poland.

Eventually, Truman and Churchill thought that they had won a major concession from Stalin: the Soviet leader agreed that the Lublin government should be expanded to include some of the London Poles and he accepted that free elections should be held as soon as possible in Poland. When asked how soon these elections could be held, Stalin replied: 'It should be possible within a month.'

> ## >> Activity
>
> Look at the Sources B and D. Summarise in your own words the details of the Yalta Agreement on Poland and Eastern Europe.

SOURCE C

Churchill, Roosevelt and Stalin at Yalta, February 1945. Their discussions centred on the future of Poland.

SOURCE D

The Yalta Agreement included specific plans for the future of Poland.

A new situation has been created in Poland as a result of her complete liberation by the Red Army. This calls for the establishment of a Polish government which can be more broadly based than was possible before the recent liberation of the Western part of Poland. The Provisional Government should therefore be re-organised on a more democratic basis with the inclusion of democratic leaders from Poland itself and from Poles abroad. This Polish government shall be pledged to the holding of free elections as soon as possible. In these elections all democratic and anti-Nazi parties shall have the right to take part and to put forward candidates.

SOURCE B

The Yalta Agreement made the following statement about the future of Eastern Europe. This became known as the Declaration on Liberated Europe:

The three governments [USA, USSR, Britain] will assist the people in any European liberated state to form interim governments broadly representative of all democratic elements in the population and pledged to the earliest possible establishment through free elections of governments responsive to the will of the people.

THE TERMS OF THE YALTA AGREEMENT

The final Agreement included a Declaration on Liberated Europe. This stated that each liberated country would be given an emergency government with representatives from any important non-fascist groups and that free elections would be held as soon as possible to set up a democratic government.

The borders of Poland were to be altered so that the USSR gained a huge amount of territory from eastern Poland. In return Poland was promised land taken from the eastern part of Germany.

The Lublin government in Poland was to be expanded so that it also included some of the London Poles. Free elections would be held in Poland as soon as possible.

The British and the Americans held many prisoners of war from Soviet territory. These were men from German-occupied lands who had chosen or been forced to join the German army. At Yalta it was agreed that they would be sent back to the USSR. About 10,000 of these men were executed on their return and many more were imprisoned.

The leaders agreed that Germany should be divided into occupied zones. Churchill argued that there should be a French zone, as well as a British, American and Soviet zone. This was because Churchill was keen to restore the power of France. Stalin and Roosevelt accepted this suggestion.

The USSR agreed to help in the war against Japan. In return the USSR gained control of island territories north of Japan. This turned out to be a very good deal for the USSR because Soviet troops did not have to do very much fighting before the Japanese surrender.

The leaders agreed to the setting up of the United Nations. Stalin successfully argued that each country should have a veto on the decisions of the powerful Security Council.

SOURCE E

One of the achievements of the Yalta conference was the decision to establish the United Nations.

>> Activity

The Yalta Conference covered many important topics and the table on this page gives a summary of the areas of agreement. Using the table and your knowledge of the background make a list of what Stalin gained from the Yalta Conference.

The weakness of the Yalta Agreement

Yalta was the high-point of the wartime alliance. To Roosevelt and many Americans it seemed like the beginning of a post-war period of co-operation. There was enthusiastic cheering in the American Senate when the Agreement was read out. In fact, the Yalta Agreement was flawed in a number of important ways:

> ### YALTA: THE PROBLEMS
>
> > The Soviets and the Americans interpreted it differently. The Agreement talked about the need for 'democracy' and 'free elections'. For Roosevelt democracy was the American system of free speech. Stalin's idea of democracy was a communist one, in which the communist party represented the people and no opposition was allowed.
>
> > Yalta raised false expectations in the USA. People expected that Stalin would now allow western-style governments to be set up in Eastern Europe. They were bitterly disappointed when this did not happen.
>
> > The Agreement tried to achieve compromise over the future of Poland. In fact, compromise was not possible. Either Poland was democratic or it was friendly towards the USSR. Leading figures in Polish society were anti-Russian. Stalin knew that he could only make sure that Poland was friendly by destroying free speech.

Yalta in practice

Roosevelt was proud of the Yalta Agreement. He was disappointed to see how Stalin put it into practice. Stalin paid only lip service to the idea of bringing non-communists into the government of Poland. At Yalta it was agreed that the Soviet Foreign Minister, Molotov, would negotiate the details of the new Polish government with the British and American ambassadors to Moscow. These talks were not successful. Molotov refused to let the London Poles play a significant part in the government. Harriman, the American ambassador, later said: 'We began to realise that Stalin's language was somewhat different from ours.' By the beginning of April Harriman was reporting to Truman that the talks had achieved nothing. At the same time Polish opponents of communism were dealt with ruthlessly. In March, 16 leaders of the Polish Resistance went, at the invitation of Stalin, to have talks with the Soviet authorities near Warsaw. They were promised their own personal safety. They were arrested and were never seen again.

SOURCE F

Roosevelt was now dying, but he managed to write a letter of criticism to Stalin:

I cannot conceal from you the concern with which I view the development of events since our fruitful meeting at Yalta. So far there has been a discouraging lack of progress made in the carrying out of the decisions we made at the Conference, particularly those relating to the Polish question. I am frankly puzzled as to why this should be and must tell you that I do not fully understand the attitude of your government.
F. D. Roosevelt, 1 April 1945

SOURCE G

Churchill was not pleased by the news from Poland. He wrote to Stalin on 29 April 1945.

The British went to war on account of Poland. They can never feel this war will have ended rightly unless Poland has a fair deal in the sense of independence and freedom, on the basis of friendship with Russia. It was on this that I thought we agreed at Yalta.

SOURCE H

Stalin refused to give any ground. In May, Stalin said the Americans were to blame for any bad feeling.

At Yalta it had been agreed that the existing government of Poland was to be reconstructed. Anyone with common sense could see that this means that the present [Lublin] government was to form the basis of the new government. No other understanding of the Yalta Agreement is possible. The Russians should not be treated as fools.

A new face at the White House

A key figure in the early stages of the Cold War was the American President, Harry Truman. It was only through chance that he became President. As Vice President he took over when Roosevelt died in April 1945. Truman was a Democrat politician from Missouri. He had made his reputation in domestic politics. He had only been Vice President for a few weeks and he had almost no experience of international politics. He was very different from Roosevelt and his personality played a part in the development of a tougher American policy. Roosevelt was much more diplomatic than Truman. Roosevelt was sure that the USA and the Soviet Union could remain friendly after the war. Just a few hours before he died Roosevelt sent a message to Churchill. The British leader had been trying to get Roosevelt to take a tough line on communist control in Poland. Roosevelt replied: 'I would minimize the general Soviet problem as much as possible.' To the last, Roosevelt remained convinced that the USA would stay on good terms with the Soviet Union. Truman was less certain about Soviet intentions.

SOURCE I

Harry Truman, the new American President, took a tougher line towards the Soviet Union than his predecessor, F. D. Roosevelt.

>> Activity

1 Explain in your own words why Roosevelt and Churchill were disappointed at the way Stalin put the Yalta Agreement into practice.

2 What evidence is there from Sources F–H, that the leaders had different interpretations of the Yalta Agreement?

Truman takes a tough line

Truman showed his different style as soon as he came to power. In April 1945 Truman spoke angrily to the Soviet Foreign Minister, Molotov. He insisted that the Soviets must carry out the Yalta Agreement and allow free elections in Poland. He would not listen to Molotov's explanations. As Molotov left he said: 'I have never been talked to like that before in my life.' To which Truman said: 'Carry out your agreements and you won't get talked to like that.'

SOURCE J

An American historian saw Truman's angry meeting with Molotov as a major step towards the start of the Cold War.

After only eleven days in power Harry Truman made his decision to lay down the law to an ally which had contributed more in blood and agony than we had – and about Poland, an area through which Russia had been invaded three times since 1914. The basis for the Cold War was laid on 23 April in the scourging which Truman administered to Molotov, giving notice that in areas of the most crucial concern to Russia our wishes must be obeyed.

D. F. Fleming, The Cold War and its Origins 1917–1960, 1961

SOURCE L

Truman described his new approach to the Soviet Union in May 1945.

We have to get tough with the Russians. They don't know how to behave. They are like bulls in a china shop. They are only twenty-five years old. We are over a hundred and the British are centuries older. We have got to teach the Russians how to behave.

The Potsdam Conference

The leaders of the USA, USSR and Britain met at Potsdam, near Berlin, between 17 July and 2 August 1945. This was the last of the great wartime summit meetings. The membership of the Conference showed that the wartime alliance was changing. At previous conferences the American leader had been Roosevelt; now it was Truman. Churchill was replaced halfway through by the Labour leader, Clement Attlee.

At Potsdam, Truman told Stalin that America had the atomic bomb. Churchill noticed the sense of power that Truman seemed to feel now that he had this powerful weapon. Later Churchill wrote: 'Truman was a changed man. He told the Russians where they got on and off and generally bossed this whole meeting.' The US government thought that it might take 20 years for the Soviet Union to develop an atom bomb. Truman believed that the bomb put the USA in a strong position in any arguments with the Soviet Union.

SOURCE K

The Allied leaders at Potsdam: Attlee, Truman and Stalin. The British and American leaders were new to their posts. Truman was determined to treat Stalin with firmness.

What was agreed at Potsdam? What were the areas of disagreement from the Potsdam discussions?

POTSDAM: AREAS OF AGREEMENT AND DISAGREEMENT

> German reparations were agreed. Each country was to take reparations from its own area of occupation. The Soviet Union was to receive some additional industrial equipment from the western zones of occupation: little of this was ever handed over.

> The details of the German–Polish borders on the rivers Oder and Neisse were finally agreed. The British and Americans disliked the position of the new border but could do little about it.

> It was agreed that the Nazi Party should be stamped out in all sectors of Germany.

> The Soviet Union wanted to play a part in the running of the rich German industrial area of the Ruhr. The USA rejected this idea.

> The Soviet Union wanted to share in the occupation of Japan. Truman firmly blocked this idea.

> The USA and Britain asked for a greater say in what went on in Eastern Europe. Stalin rejected this suggestion.

SOURCE M

Winston Churchill was the former British Prime Minister. He lost power in the 1945 general election. He made the famous 'iron curtain' speech in March 1946.

From Stettin in the Baltic, to Trieste in the Adriatic, an iron curtain has descended across the continent. Behind that line lie all the capitals of the ancient states of Central and Eastern Europe: Warsaw, Berlin, Prague, Vienna, Budapest, Bucharest and Sofia. All these famous cities lie in the Soviet sphere, and all are subject to a high and increasing control from Moscow. The Russian-dominated Polish government has been encouraged to make enormous and wrongful inroads upon Germany, and mass expulsions of millions of Germans are now taking place. The Communist Parties, which were very small in all of these Eastern states, are seeking everywhere to obtain totalitarian control.

The Iron Curtain

The new hostility towards the Soviet Union was encouraged by Winston Churchill in a famous speech on 5 March 1946. The speech was made at Fulton, Missouri. President Truman was in the audience and had seen the speech before it was given. Churchill called for an American–British alliance to meet the communist menace. At first some Americans felt that he was exaggerating. Gradually most Americans came to agree with him.

>> Activity

Look back at this unit. Explain in your own words how each of the following factors made the Cold War more likely:

a long-term hostility between the USA and the Soviet Union;

b arguments over the Yalta Agreements;

c the personality of Truman.

The Soviet take-over of Eastern Europe

After 1945 the Soviet Union took control of much of Eastern Europe. Historians are still debating the motives behind this take-over. Was this a defensive move or was this a step towards a take-over of the whole of Europe?

Why did Stalin take control of Eastern Europe?

Liberation?

The Soviet take-over was not complete until 1948 but it began before the end of the Second World War. As the Red Army drove the Germans westwards the Soviet leadership made sure that territory came under the control of people friendly to the Soviets. In most countries the Soviet government set up anti-fascist coalition governments, but gave local communists a leading position. These communist-dominated governments introduced nationalisation and took land away from the landlords. Opposition parties were gradually undermined. Elections were rigged. Eventually all opposition was destroyed and Soviet control was complete. The process was more rapid in some countries than in others.

THE SOVIET TAKE-OVER OF EASTERN EUROPE

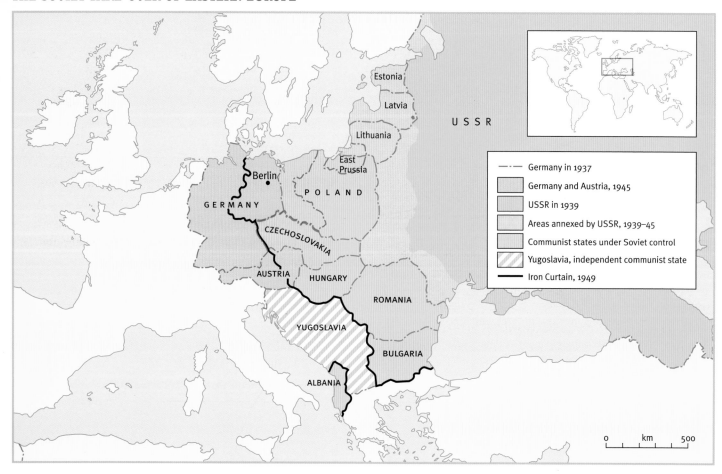

Legend:
- Germany in 1937
- Germany and Austria, 1945
- USSR in 1939
- Areas annexed by USSR, 1939–45
- Communist states under Soviet control
- Yugoslavia, independent communist state
- Iron Curtain, 1949

Look at the following information about the stages of the Soviet take-over. How did the Soviet Union take control of Eastern Europe?

STAGE 1: THE TAKE-OVER OF POLAND

As we have seen, Stalin's first priority was control of Poland. At the end of June 1945 a few London Poles were included in the Polish government. However, it remained completely dominated by the communists of the Lublin group. The Western allies admitted defeat over Poland by 'recognising' the largely communist government on 5 July 1945. This meant that Britain and the USA accepted that the communists were in charge in Warsaw. Communist power was strengthened even further in January 1947 when rigged elections were held in Poland. The leader of the London Poles, Mikolaczyk, thought his life was in danger and fled the country.

STAGE 2: THE TAKE-OVER OF ROMANIA AND BULGARIA

After Poland, Stalin's immediate priorities were the control of Romania and Bulgaria. Look at the map; can you work out why these three countries were important to Stalin? As the Red Army swept into Bulgaria and Romania in late 1944 coalition governments dominated by communists were set up. In February 1945, within days of the Yalta agreement, a top Soviet politician, Andrei Vyshinsky, ordered the King of Romania to appoint a new prime minister chosen by Stalin. When the King said that this was not in line with the Yalta agreement, Vyshinsky slammed his fist on the table and shouted at the King. Stalin got his prime minister. By the middle of 1945 communists were in firm control in Romania. Elections took place in Bulgaria in November. These elections were rigged and the communist Fatherland Front won. In September 1946 the communist government in Bulgaria abolished the monarchy. The monarchy in Romania was abolished in 1947.

STAGE 3: THE TAKE-OVER OF HUNGARY AND CZECHOSLOVAKIA

In contrast with Poland, Romania and Bulgaria Stalin did not at first have a clear view of what he wanted for Hungary and Czechoslovakia. He allowed free elections to take place in Hungary in November 1945. The non-communist Smallholders' Party was the most successful party. Fresh elections were held in August 1947. This time the elections were rigged and an exclusively communist government took power. In November all non-communist parties were banned.

The final stage in the take-over came when communists seized power in Czechoslovakia in 1948. Before that the country was ruled by a coalition of communists and non-communists. This was the one country in Eastern Europe with a strong local communist party. There were fair elections in 1946 and the communists won 38 per cent of the vote. The President, Beneš, was a non-communist while Gottwald, the Prime Minister, was a communist. The Foreign Minister, Jan Masaryk, was also a non-communist. There was an economic crisis in the country from mid-1947. The harvest was bad and industry was in trouble. Elections were due for May 1948. The communists were afraid that they would do badly. The communists used armed force to seize power. Many non-communists were arrested and Masaryk was murdered. Rigged elections were held shortly afterwards and the communists won a huge majority. The Soviet take-over was complete.

The war as a triumph for Soviet communism

The Soviet leaders felt that their country had made by far the most important contribution to the winning of the war. The British and the Americans had helped, but Stalin believed, with some justification, that the Soviet Union had cut the heart out of the German army. 10 million Germans, who represented 80 per cent of German losses, died on the Eastern Front. The Soviet leaders believed their country had largely won the war, so they had a right to shape the future of Europe.

Stalin also saw the war as proof that communism worked: in the battle to the death between communist Russia and capitalist Germany, communism had triumphed. This gave a new sense of confidence and determination to the Soviet government.

Never again: the level of the Soviet wartime sacrifice

The Soviet Union suffered much more than the other allies during the war. This made a difference to attitudes after the war. About 15 million Soviet soldiers and civilians had been killed by the Germans. In addition, many people had died because of shortages of food and the other harsh conditions of wartime. As many as 25 million Soviet citizens may have died because of the war. Stalin was determined that this should never be allowed to happen again.

Soviet strategic thinking

How could the Soviet Union ensure that the devastation of the Second World War was not repeated? In 1914 and 1941 Germany had attacked Russia through Poland. In 1945 Stalin thought that sooner or later there could be yet another attack through Poland. To stop this he was determined to control Poland and other East European states. Before the Second World War these countries had been independent. Almost all of them had been governed by right-wing, anti-communist leaders. In Moscow it seemed quite likely that if the countries of Eastern Europe were again allowed to be independent, the states would again become anti-Soviet.

US imperialism?

The USA was by far the wealthiest country in the world in 1945. The Soviet government was convinced that American business leaders were planning to spread their power and increase their profits by buying up companies in other countries and selling American goods wherever they could. In this way the USA could build up a new kind of world empire. American troops would not need to conquer new lands: American capitalism would do it instead. As good communists it was the job of the Soviet leaders to try to stop American businesses from dominating the world. The setting up of a group of friendly communist countries was one way of doing this.

SOURCE A

The devastated landscape of Stalingrad at the end of the war. The Soviet Union suffered far greater damage than any other country.

Stalin's motives

Focus

Look at Sources B–F. What can we learn from them about the Stalin's motives at the end of the Second World War? Can you find evidence that:

a Stalin wanted a barrier to stop the Soviet Union from being invaded in the future;

b Stalin did not trust the Americans;

c Stalin believed in communism and thought that every country should be communist.

SOURCE E

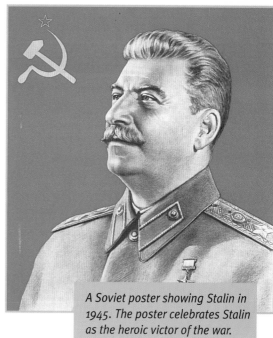

A Soviet poster showing Stalin in 1945. The poster celebrates Stalin as the heroic victor of the war.

SOURCE B

Stalin speaking on 9 February 1945:

Victory means, first of all, that our Soviet social system has won. The Soviet social system has successfuly stood the test in the fire of war and it has proved its complete vitality. The Soviet social system has proved to be more capable and more stable than a non-Soviet social system. The Soviet social system is a better form of society than any non-Soviet social system.

SOURCE C

At Yalta, in February 1945, Stalin tried to explain to Churchill and Roosevelt why Poland was so important to the Soviet Union.

Mr Churchill has said that for Great Britain the Polish question is one of honour. But for the Russians it is a question both of honour and security. Throughout history Poland has been the corridor for attack on Russia. It is not merely a question of honour for Russia, but one of life and death.

SOURCE D

In May 1945 Stalin was worried at the end of the war in Europe and felt unhappy at the approach of the new US president, Harry Truman.

The Soviet government is alarmed by the attitude of the US government. The American attitude cooled once it became clear that Germany was defeated. It was as though the Americans were saying that the Russians were no longer needed.

SOURCE F

In March 1946, Stalin replied to Churchill's famous speech about the 'iron curtain':

It should not be forgotten that the Germans invaded the USSR through Finland, Poland, Rumania, Bulgaria and Hungary. The Germans were able to invade because governments hostile to the Soviet Union existed in these countries. As a result the Soviet Union had a loss of life several times greater than that of Britain and the United States put together. Some people may be able to forget the huge sacrifices of the Soviet people but the Soviet Union cannot forget them. And so what is surprising about the fact that the Soviet Union, anxious for its future safety, is trying to see that governments loyal to the Soviet Union should exist in these countries? How can anyone who has not taken total leave of his senses describe these peaceful wishes of the Soviet Union as expansionist tendencies on the part of the Soviet Union?

>> Activity

It has been argued that Stalin took over Eastern Europe as the first stage towards a communist take-over of the world. Does the information in this unit support this explanation? Explain your answer in detail.

The Truman Doctrine and the Marshall Plan

The government of the USA was deeply unhappy at the spread of communism to Eastern Europe. Traditionally American foreign policy was based on isolationism: having as little to do as possible with international politics. The Soviet take-over forced American politicians to think again and to reject traditional thinking.

How did the USA react to the Soviet take-over of Eastern Europe?

After 1945 the USA moved away from isolationism and became active throughout the world. Eventually the USA built up its own 'sphere of interest': a group of pro-American states that included all of the world's richest industrialised countries.

1946: Cold War attitudes develop

Relations between the USA and the Soviet Union deteriorated throughout 1946:

> The Americans were very critical of Soviet policy in Iran. Soviet troops were in the north of Persia, now Iran, at the end of the war. Under wartime agreements they were supposed to withdraw in March 1946. The US government suspected that this was the first step towards a Soviet take-over of part of Iran. They criticised the Soviet occupation at the United Nations. Stalin gave in and withdrew his troops.

> The Council of Foreign Ministers met in Paris in April 1946. The American representative, Byrnes, blocked every Soviet proposal and criticised Soviet policy in Eastern Europe.

> The Soviet navy wished to send ships through the Black Sea Straits and to set up naval bases in the area. Turkey felt threatened by these plans and in August 1946 the US government blocked the Soviet plans. The Americans made it clear that they would use force to resist any Soviet move. American warships were sent to the area to warn off the Soviets.

The crisis of 1947

American policy took shape in the crucial year of 1947. At the beginning of the year there was an economic crisis in Western Europe. The harvest in 1946 was poor and there was food shortage in many places. The winter was unusually fierce and people were cold as well as hungry. In Britain unemployment was soaring and food rationing was more severe than it had been during the war. In Germany people were close to starvation. Millions of refugees had fled to western Germany and this added to the shortage of fuel, food and jobs. In France and Italy discontent led to massive support for the local communist parties; unless conditions improved there was a real possibility that the communists could come to power. By early 1947 it was clear to the US government that their friends in Western Europe could not cope alone. Some Americans had hoped that the return of peace would allow the USA to go back to its isolationist policy. Truman and his advisers realised that this was not possible.

The Truman Doctrine

In February 1947 the British government sent a dramatic message to Washington – Britain could no longer afford to pay for troops in Greece and Turkey. Unless America replaced Britain in Greece and Turkey these countries could easily come under Soviet control. Truman decided to offer American financial help to Greece and Turkey. He went further and declared that American support was available for any people who wanted to fight communism. This became known as the Truman Doctrine. It was based on the idea of containment – the USA would use its wealth and power to stop or contain the spread of communism.

SOURCE A

Truman announced his 'doctrine' in a speech to the US Congress on 12 March 1947.

At the present moment in world history nearly every nation must choose between alternative ways of life. One way of life is based upon the will of the majority, and is distinguished by free institutions, representative government, free elections, guarantees of individual liberty, freedom of speech and religion and freedom from political oppression.

The second way of life is based upon the will of a minority forcibly imposed upon the majority. It relies upon terror and oppression, a controlled press and radio, fixed elections and the suppression of personal freedom.

I believe it must be the policy of the United States to support people who are resisting attempted subjugation by armed minorities or by outside pressures. I believe that we must help free peoples to work out their own destiny in their own way.

Through the Truman Doctrine, the USA had rejected 'isolationism'. America had announced to the world that it would play a leading part in world politics. In Greece and Turkey the doctrine was successful. The communist side was defeated in the Greek Civil War by 1949, and Turkey remained part of the Western pro-American group of countries. Initially, 'the doctrine' was applied in Europe and the Middle East. Eventually, it was extended to the whole world and led to war in Korea and Vietnam.

SOURCE B

A scene from the Greek Civil War: an anti-communist soldier guards communist suspects. Truman intervened to make sure that the communists lost the war. This was the beginning of the Truman Doctrine.

>> Activity

What was the Truman Doctrine? How was the Doctrine different to the traditional American policy of isolationism?

The Marshall Plan

Another strand of American policy emerged in 1947. In Washington there was a belief that communism could only be stopped if Western Europe became wealthy. By the spring of 1947 it was clear that without American help there was little chance of economic recovery.

SOURCE C

Will Clayton, a leading American politician, was sent to Europe in May 1947 to report on conditions.

Millions of people in the cities are slowly starving. Without further prompt and substantial aid from the US, economic and political dislocation will overwhelm Europe.

The USA decided to offer massive economic aid to Western Europe. The project was organised by the American Secretary of State, General George Marshall, and was known as the Marshall Plan. Marshall announced his scheme in a speech at Harvard University in June 1947.

A large amount of American money was made available to those European countries which made an acceptable application. The Soviet Union was, in theory, able to apply for help. However, Stalin saw the plan as an attempt to impose capitalist ideas on European countries. He refused to have anything to do with it. The governments of Poland and Czechoslovkia wanted to join the Marshall Plan but Stalin ordered them not to take part. Stalin was right in thinking that Marshall Plan money would be tied to American-style ideas. The Plan was based on a belief that communism would be much less attractive to ordinary people if they had good jobs and were well paid.

SOURCE D

The American politician, Vandenburg, speaking in 1948, made it clear that the Marshall Plan was part of a strategy to stop the spread of communism.

The Plan is a calculated risk to help stop World War III before it starts. The area covered by the Plan contains 270,000,000 people of the stock which largely made America. This vast friendly segment of the earth must not collapse. The iron curtain must not come to the rims of the Atlantic.

Leaders of 16 West European countries met in Paris between July and September 1947 and wrote a recovery plan. The military governors of western Germany took part. The US accepted the plan and the first American money was transferred. The Marshall Plan was a step towards the division of Germany and this angered the Soviet authorities. Economically, the western area of Germany was now functioning as if it was a separate country from the eastern sector.

The Plan was a great success. Over four years, $13,000 million of help was provided. European countries were encouraged to reduce import taxes and this increased the level of trade. By 1952, when the Marshall Plan officially ended, the countries of Western Europe were well on the road to a period of great economic prosperity. The Plan was also very useful to the USA. By rebuilding Western Europe, America was creating wealthy trade partners who would want to buy large amounts of American goods.

SOURCE E

A Soviet anti-Marshall Plan poster depicting American aid as a menacing influence on the world.

The Soviet response

The Soviet Union organised an international conference in September 1947 in order to condemn the Truman Doctrine and the Marshall Plan. A new organisation was set up to strengthen the links between communist parties in different countries. It was called Cominform (The Communist Information Bureau).

SOURCE F

At the Cominform Conference in September 1947 the Soviet leader, A. A. Zhdanov, bitterly attacked the Truman Doctrine and the Marshall Plan.

The Truman Doctrine and the Marshall Plan are both part of an American plan to enslave Europe. The United States has launched an attack on the principle of each nation being in charge of its own affairs. By contrast, the Soviet Union is tireless in upholding the principle of real equality and independence among nations whatever their size. The Soviet Union will make every effort to ensure that the Marshall Plan is doomed to failure. The communist parties of France, Italy, Great Britain and other countries must play a part in this.

Comecon

Having failed to destroy the Marshall Plan, the USSR created its own economic bloc of countries in Eastern Europe. In January 1949 Comecon (the Council for Mutual Economic Aid) was set up. It was a trading organisation of communist countries but was nowhere near as successful as the Marshall Plan. It did not involve any injection of money into East European countries. Eventually the Soviet Union used it to encourage each country to specialise in different products.

>> Activity

1 What was the Truman Doctrine?

2 What was the Marshall Plan?

3 How did the Soviet Union react to the Truman Doctrine and the Marshall Plan?

Communists in Western countries were told to try to wreck the Marshall Plan through strikes. There were very large communist parties in France and Italy. In the winter of 1947–8 communist workers in these two countries organised a series of strikes and demonstrations. This attempt to wreck the Marshall Plan did not work. Despite the strikes, American money flowed into Western Europe and eventually the strikes came to an end.

SOURCE G

Italian soldiers arrest a lorry-load of communist activists during industrial unrest in 1948. The communists were organising strikes in order to wreck the Marshall Plan.

American motives at the start of the Cold War

The American government responded very energetically to the Soviet take-over in Eastern Europe. The Truman Plan and the Marshall Plan signalled a new stage in the developing Cold War.

Why was the US government hostile towards the Soviet Union?

The world's leading nation

The USA was well-placed to play a leading part in world affairs after 1945. It was in excellent economic condition, unlike almost every other powerful country. At the end of the war the defeated nations of Germany and Japan lay in ruins. Several of the 'winners' also faced great difficulties. Britain and France were in debt and were selling very few goods abroad. As a result they could no longer afford to maintain huge armed forces. Much of the Soviet Union was wrecked by the war. By contrast, the rich USA became even richer in the war years. The output of American factories increased by 50 per cent during the war. By 1945 half of all the manufactured goods in the world were made in the USA. One third of all the world's exports came from the USA. Money flooded in and in 1945 the USA held almost two-thirds of all the gold reserves in the world.

As the leaders of the world's richest and most successful country, American politicians were very confident and expected to have a major say in the way the world was run. Leading Americans were extremely proud of their country and believed that American-style capitalism and free trade was the way forward for all other countries. They were, therefore, annoyed by Soviet communists who tried to stop the spread of American business and said that American capitalism was wicked.

SOURCE A

An advertisement of the late 1940s illustrates the relatively high standard of living enjoyed by many Americans. As the elderly couple cook a meal in their comfortable house, their son arrives in his brand-new car. American leaders were very proud of their economic prosperity.

The nuclear monopoly

The USA was not only rich, it was also powerful. With 1,200 major warships and over 2,000 heavy bombers it had the strongest navy and airforce in the world. The American feeling of power was greatly increased when the atomic bomb was produced in 1945. No other country had this immensely powerful weapon. The Soviet Union produced an atom bomb in 1949, but in 1945 Americans thought that it could be 20 years before any other country caught up with their atomic power. American politicians took a more aggressive line towards the Soviet Union because they thought they could use the bomb as a threat. (This overestimated the importance of the atomic bomb. Stalin rightly thought that the bomb was so terrible that the Americans would hardly ever dare to use it.)

SOURCE B

An American atom bomb test. Until 1949 the USA had a monopoly of the atom bomb and this gave the Americans a sense of superiority over the Soviet Union.

Memories of the 1930s

At the start of 1946 there was a strong feeling in Washington that the US government needed to take a tough line with the USSR. Talks were getting nowhere and Truman became convinced that only the threat of force would stop the Soviets from taking over more land. In January Truman told his advisers that he wanted the USSR to be faced with an 'iron fist'. He added, 'I'm tired of babying the Soviets'.

This hard-line approach was greatly influenced by recent memories. The world had been through great turmoil in the 1930s. In Washington it seemed that the causes of the problem were:

> the rise of evil dictators like Hitler

> the economic crisis of the pre-war Depression.

People in Washington thought that they needed to stop the rise of any more wicked dictators like Hitler. During the war most Americans had a positive view of Stalin. Soon after the war the American Press portrayed him, like Hitler, as a monster and a dictator. The lesson of the 1930s was that appeasement did not work with such people. It would therefore be disastrous if Americans made any concessions to the Soviet Union.

There was also an economic reason for taking a tough line on communism. American politicians were terrified at the idea that there could be another Depression like the one in the early 1930s. Another Depression could only be avoided if American factories were busy. American business was the engine of the world economy and it needed new markets in which to sell its goods. Communist countries were unlikely to buy many American goods. So the spread of communism was a threat to the American economy.

George Kennan and the 'long telegram'

One American expert played a crucial part in encouraging a hostile attitude towards the Soviet Union. His name was George Kennan. In February 1946 Kennan sent a famous report to Washington. He was based at the time at the American Embassy in Moscow and his report gave the American government a detailed view of Soviet motives. The report became known as 'the long telegram'. It made a big impact in Washington. The US government accepted Kennan's views and published hundreds of copies of the telegram for its officials to read. Kennan said that the Soviet government was determined to expand and must be stopped. Kennan also developed the idea of 'containment'. The theory of containment was that the USA should use all means, including the threat of force, to stop Soviet power spreading any further. The USA became committed to containment and this remained its policy until the end of the Cold War in the late 1980s.

SOURCE D

A summary of George Kennan's 'long telegram', February 1946:

> Soviet policy is a continuation of traditional Russian policy of hostility towards the outside world.

> Russian leaders today, as in the past, feel threatened and insecure because they know that the West is more advanced. In order to remove the threat, Russian leaders are determined to destroy the Western world.

> Communism has made matters worse. Marxist ideas encourage the Soviet leaders to be absolutely ruthless.

> The Soviet Union will use every method possible to smash democracy in the Western world.

> The Soviet leaders are fanatics and can never be trusted.

SOURCE C

George Kennan. He was a young diplomat based in Moscow in the war. He persuaded many people in the American government of the need for a tough line against the Soviet Union.

SOURCE E

A Soviet poster of the 1940s shows the different ethnic groups of the Soviet Union united by communism. Americans were afraid that Soviet communists wanted to spread their revolutionary ideas throughout the world.

How many different reasons can you find in the following sources to explain why the USA was hostile towards the Soviet Union?

SOURCE F

In 1945 the American ambassador in Moscow commented on the differences between the USA and the Soviet Union.

I am afraid that Stalin does not, and never will, fully understand our interest in free Poland as a matter of principle. It is hard for him to appreciate our faith in principles. It is difficult for him to understand why we should want to interfere with Soviet policy in a country like Poland, which he considers so important to Russia's security, unless we have some ulterior motive.

Averell Harriman

SOURCE G

The US diplomat, George Kennan, in February 1946 said that Soviet leaders wanted to destroy the American way of life.

All Soviet efforts will be negative and destructive in character, designed to tear down sources of strength beyond reach of Soviet control. We have here a political force committed fanatically to the belief that with the US there can be no permanent way of living peacefully together. If Soviet power is to be secure our traditonal way of life must be destroyed and the international authority of our state destroyed.

SOURCE H

Senator E. Johnson made this speech in November 1945:

We can drop, at a moment's notice, atomic bombs on any spot on earth. With vision and guts and plenty of atomic bombs the United States can outlaw wars of aggression.

SOURCE I

President Truman wrote this letter in January 1946:

There isn't a doubt in my mind that Russia intends an invasion of Turkey and the seizure of the Black Sea Straits on the Mediterranean. Unless Russia is faced with an iron fist and strong language another war is in the making. Only one language do they understand: 'How many divisions have you?'

SOURCE J

The American General Eisenhower became President in 1953. In 1951 he commented on American motives.

From my viewpoint, foreign policy is based primarily on one consideration: the need for the US to obtain raw materials and to preserve profitable foreign markets. Out of this comes the need to make certain that those areas of the world where there are essential raw materials are accessible to us.

SOURCE K

William C. Bullitt was a politician and former American diplomat. He made this speech in 1947:

The Soviet Union's assault upon the West is about at the stage of Hitler's manoeuvring into Czechoslovakia. The final aim of Russia is world conquest.

>> Activity

Why was the US government keen to confront the Soviet Union after 1945? In your answer you should mention:

> the wealth and self-confidence of Americans after the war

> the initial monopoly of the atomic bomb

> memories of appeasement

> the influence of George Kennan.

The Berlin Blockade and NATO

In 1948 Stalin tried to starve the people of West Berlin into submission. He failed. The Western allies kept West Berlin supplied through a massive airlift.

What were the consequences of the Berlin Blockade?

Towards a divided Germany

By early 1948 Stalin had control of much of Eastern Europe. The Americans responded by helping to make Western Europe wealthy and pro-American. As part of this process the division of Germany became more and more permanent. The west of Germany had long been the industrial heartland of continental Europe. The US government decided to include western Germany in its plans for a new non-communist Western Europe.

News of a new currency for the west of Germany alarmed Stalin. He saw it as another step towards a divided Germany with the wealthier, larger part of the country closely allied to the USA. Stalin was worried by the idea of a successful, anti-communist government in the west of Germany. In his mind it raised the possibility of another German attack on Russia, as in 1914 and 1941.

In attempting to stop the formation of West Germany, Stalin thought he had one powerful weapon. West Berlin was controlled by the American, French and British forces – but it was a western 'island' deep inside the Soviet sector of Germany. Soviet forces controlled all the land routes into West Berlin. Over 2 million people lived in West Berlin and Stalin could cut off their supplies by simply closing the roads and the railways. As a protest against the currency reforms and the moves towards a divided Germany Stalin decided to put a blockade on West Berlin.

THE EMERGENCE OF WEST GERMANY

> The Marshall Plan for the economic rebuilding of Europe was extended to the western part of Germany but not to the Soviet zone.

> In January 1947 the British and the American governments fused their two zones of Germany into a single administrative unit that was known at the time as Bizonia. In many ways this was the beginning of the establishment of West Germany.

> In June 1948 the Western allies introduced a new currency into their area of control. The new money, known as the Deutschmark, was not used in the Soviet zone.

GERMANY 1945–7

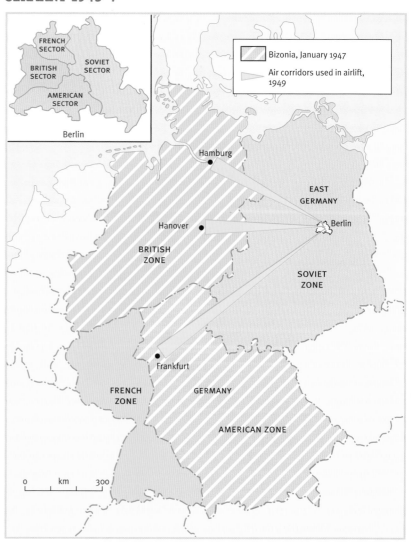

SOURCE A

The blockade began on 23 June 1948 when the Soviet authorities made this announcement:

The transport division of the Soviet Military Administration is compelled to halt all the passenger and freight traffic to and from Berlin at 06.00 hours because of technical difficulties.

The Berlin Airlift

The Western allies were taken by surprise at the start of the blockade. The Americans were initially not sure how to respond. Some advisers thought that the Western powers would have to give way because the 2 million people in West Berlin would starve as long as the roads out of Berlin remained blocked. Another view was that tanks should be used to blast a way through the blockade. The leading American military expert, General Clay, was keen to send his troops down the autobahn towards Berlin. This could easily have led to a full-scale war with the USSR. The government decided on a middle course: not to provoke war by sending troops towards Berlin but to keep the city supplied by aircraft. Never before had a huge besieged city been kept going by an airlift.

SOURCE B

A month after the start of the blockade, Truman ordered General Clay to report to him in Washington to review the Berlin question. In his memoirs, Truman recalled the meeting with Clay on 22 July 1948:

Clay said that the abandonment of Berlin would have a disastrous effect upon our plans for Western Germany. It would also slow down European recovery. The [West] Germans were concerned about the possibility of our leaving Berlin. We should go to any lengths to find a peaceful solution to the situation, but we had to remain in Berlin. He reported that the airlift was more than enough to meet food requirements, but was inadequate to include the necessary amounts of coal.

I asked General Clay if there were any indications that the Russians would go to war. He said he did not think so. What they seemed to be aiming at was to score a major victory by forcing us out of Berlin, either now or after winter weather forced us to curtail the airlift.

I directed the Air Force to furnish the fullest support possible to the problem of supplying Berlin.

SOURCE C

Children from West Berlin watch a US cargo plane bringing in supplies to the besieged city during the Berlin Blockade.

To people in the West, Stalin seemed to be acting with extreme aggression. The attack on Berlin looked like the first step towards a communist march westwards. The Western allies acted firmly in carrying out the airlift. To President Truman it was a test of the new policy of containment: the USSR could not be allowed to take over West Berlin.

>> Activity

Explain in your own words why Stalin decided to impose a blockade on West Berlin.

Stalin ends the siege

Eventually Stalin had to admit that his attempt to starve out West Berlin had failed. In May 1949 the Soviet authorities called off the blockade. The airlift was a triumph for the American and British air forces. During the airlift British and US planes flew nearly 200,000 missions to Berlin. At the end of the blockade the airport in West Berlin was handling an enormous 1,000 arrivals and departures every day. Over 1.5 million tons of food, fuel and equipment was sent in to Berlin. This achievement clearly proved how determined the USA was to resist Stalin. The Berlin airlift showed how far international politics had changed since 1945. Berlin had then been a symbol of defeated Nazism. By 1948 it was a symbol of Western freedom and the struggle with communism.

SOURCE D

Konrad Adenauer, 1949. The blockade strengthened the position of conservative anti-communists like Adenauer. This was the exact opposite of what Stalin wanted when he began the Blockade.

After the blockade: the formation of West Germany

Stalin's attempt to put a stop to the creation of West Germany was a complete failure. The blockade accelerated moves towards a powerful, pro-Western state in much of Germany. As the airlift began, the military authorities in the western zones also organised meetings to work out a constitution for West Germany. The new state was called the Federal Republic of Germany and it was formally founded in May 1949. The Soviet Union responded to this by setting up a new constitution for East Germany. In October 1949 the eastern state was officially established and it was known as the German Democratic Republic.

West Germany held its first elections in August 1949. A political party called the Christian Democrats won the greatest number of seats and dominated the new state. Its leader was Konrad Adenauer, a conservative who hated communism and believed very strongly in linking West Germany to the USA and Western Europe. The development of West Germany under Adenauer was the last thing that Stalin wanted. The idea of a powerful capitalist German state made him feel insecure.

After the blockade: the formation of NATO

The blockade also encouraged the Western allies to form the North Atlantic Treaty Organisation (NATO).

SOURCE E

The North Atlantic Treaty Organisation was set up in April 1949. This is an extract from the treaty.

The Parties to this treaty agree that an armed attack against one or more of them in Europe or North America shall be considered an attack against them all. They agree that, if such an armed attack occurs, each of them will assist by taking such action as it deems necessary, including the use of armed force.

The alliance was dominated by the USA. American influence has been reflected in the fact that every single supreme commander of NATO has been an American. The formation of NATO was a milestone in American foreign policy. Never before had the USA been a member of a peacetime military alliance. The fact that Truman broke with all the traditions of American foreign policy shows how determined he was to stop the spread of communism.

NATO was more than a promise of American help in case of emergency. The alliance was to be supported with large numbers of troops on the ground. In particular, there was a large build-up of NATO forces in West Germany. By 1953, five divisions of US troops were permanently based in Germany.

The Soviet Union felt threatened by this. The sense of threat increased in 1955 when West Germany joined NATO. The Soviet Union responded by setting up its own military alliance in 1955. This was established under a treaty called the Warsaw Pact. For the next three decades NATO and Warsaw Pact forces faced each other and prepared for war.

>> Activity

1 How did the Berlin Blockade end? Was this a victory for the Soviet Union or for the USA?

2 How did the blockade speed up the formation of West Germany?

3 How did the blockade lead to the setting up of NATO?

4 Do you think that Stalin was pleased with the consequences of the Berlin Blockade?

NATO AND THE WARSAW PACT

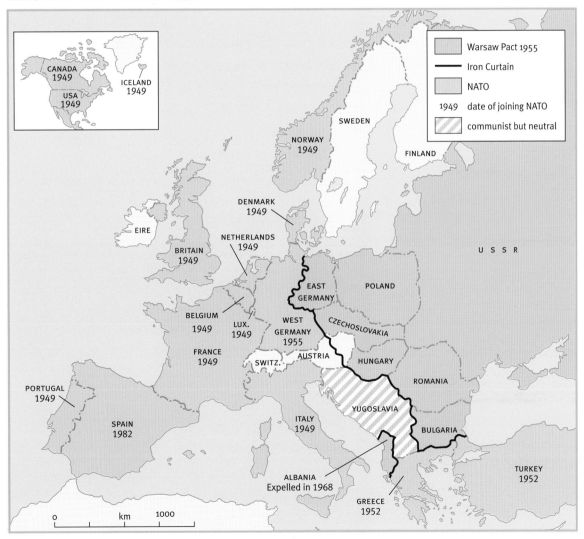

The start of the Cold War

The wartime allies become enemies

Soon after the end of the war the USA and the USSR became hostile towards each other. A period of hostility known as the Cold War lasted until the late 1980s.

YALTA AND POTSDAM

The leaders of the USA, USSR and Britain met twice in 1945 to talk about the world after the war. They had met once before in Tehran, 1943.

Yalta, February 1945

Leaders present: Roosevelt (USA), Stalin (USSR), Churchill (Britain)

Discussed: Poland and the rest of Eastern Europe

Agreed: non-communists to be part of emergency governments

free elections as soon as possible

Outcome: Soviet Union did not allow democracy in Poland

great bitterness caused in the USA

Potsdam, July 1945

Leaders present: Truman (USA), Stalin (USSR), Churchill, replaced by Attlee (Britain).

Discussed: the future running of Germany

Agreed: borders between Germany and Poland wiping out Nazi influence arrangements for reparations

Outcome: USA prevented Soviet Union involvement in the rich Ruhr area of Germany and occupied Japan

The Soviet Union blocked American involvement in Eastern Europe

The Soviet take-over

In 1946 Churchill described how an 'iron curtain' was being put across Europe; the iron curtain divided Soviet-style states in Eastern Europe from democratic, capitalist states in Western Europe. Between 1945 and 1948 the Soviet Union imposed communist governments on several East European countries:

> Poland

> Bulgaria

> Romania

> Hungary

> Czechoslovakia

The communist coup in Czechoslovakia in 1948 particularly angered people in the West.

For the Soviet leader, Stalin, the take-over was a defensive move: an attempt to build up a friendly buffer between the USSR and the Western capitalist states.

For the American leader, Truman, the take-over was an offensive move: the first step in a Soviet attempt to impose communism on all the countries of the world.

A US atomic test taking place in the Pacific Ocean near Bikini Atoll on 25 July 1946.

The American response

Between 1945 and 1949 the Americans developed a policy called 'containment'. This involved using the power and wealth of the USA to try to stop or 'contain' the spread of communism, first of all in Europe and later throughout the world.

CONTAINMENT IN EUROPE

1947: The Truman Doctrine

The American President Truman said that the world was being divided into free, democratic countries and undemocratic communist states. Truman promised help for any people who wanted to resist communism and immediate help to anti-communist governments in Greece and Turkey.

1947: The Marshall Plan

The economy of Europe was in ruins at the end of the war. The Marshall Plan, named after General George Marshall, the US Secretary of State, aimed to re-build the European economy so that it could resist communism. In theory, East European countries could join but the Americans made it clear that communist states were not welcome.

1949: the founding of NATO

The USA took the lead in organising a military alliance of non-communist countries in Europe and North America. It was called the North Atlantic Treaty Organisation. All members agreed to defend each other in case of Soviet attack.

1949: the setting up of West Germany

At the end of the war Germany was divided into the British, French, American and Soviet zones. The city of Berlin was also divided into four zones. At first both the USA and the USSR wanted a unified Germany. When the Soviet Union took control of much of Eastern Europe, America moved towards the setting up of a pro-Western state in the British, French and American zones. West Germany, officially known as the Federal Republic of Germany, was established in May 1949.

THE SOVIET REACTION TO CONTAINMENT

Stalin, in turn, saw American actions after 1945 as aggressive and a threat to the Soviet Union. The Soviet response was as follows:

1948–1949: the Berlin Blockade

West Berlin was an island of democracy and capitalism in the Soviet zone. Stalin was worried by the possibility of a strong West German state. In June 1948 Stalin blocked all road and rail transport with West Berlin. This was a failure. Britain and the USA organised an unprecedented airlift to stop West Berliners from being starved out. The blockade was ended in May 1949. The blockade accelerated moves towards a separate West Germany and the NATO alliance.

1949: COMECON

In January 1949 the Soviet Union tried to answer the Marshall Plan by setting up a trading bloc of communist countries. It was called the Council for Mutual Economic Aid or COMECON.

1949: the setting up of East Germany

After the official establishment of West Germany the Soviet zone of Germany was turned into a separate communist state, officially known as the German Democratic Republic.

1949: the Soviet atom bomb

The USA had a monopoly of atomic weapons after 1945. Stalin ordered Soviet scientists to produce an atomic bomb and in 1949 they succeeded.

1955: the Warsaw Pact

In 1955 NATO was expanded to include West Germany. The Soviet Union created a military alliance of communist countries known as the Warsaw Pact.

The Korean War

The Truman Doctrine stated that the USA would help people to fight against communism. In 1950 the USA showed that this was more than words: US troops went to war to stop the spread of communism in Korea.

How successful was the USA in the Korean War?

THE KOREAN WAR

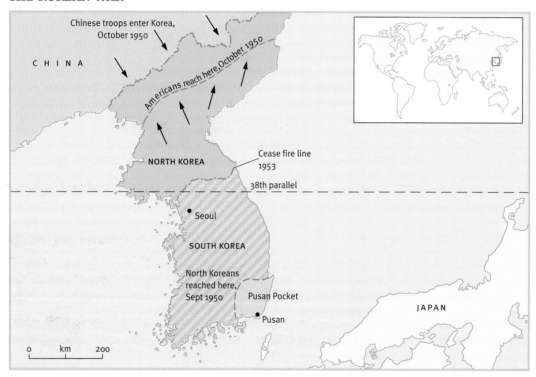

A divided land

The Japanese controlled Korea between 1904 and 1945. At the end of the Second World War Korea was in a situation similar to Germany. Russian forces were in the north of Korea and American troops had landed in the south. Korea became divided in two at the 38th parallel. In 1948 separate Korean governments were set up in the north and south of the country.

A communist, Kim Il Sung, took power in the North. From 1948 the President of South Korea was the anti-communist, Syngman Rhee. He was a corrupt leader and he soon became very unpopular. In April 1950 Rhee did badly in elections. Many of the people of the south voted in favour of unification with the communist state of the north.

Invasion

On 25 June 1950 North Korean troops invaded the South in a bid to re-unite Korea by force. Historians disagree about whether the North Koreans were told to invade by the Russians. Truman believed that the Russians were behind the attack and that it was a test of the US policy of containing communism. The invasion came at a time when many Americans were extremely worried about the challenge of communism. China had recently become a communist state. In September 1949 the Americans found out that the USSR had nuclear weapons. American politicians became convinced that communists wanted to take over the world. On hearing the news from Korea, Truman immediately ordered US forces in Japan, led by General MacArthur, to help South Korea.

Truman asked the United Nations Security Council to back the use of American troops in Korea. At that time the Soviet Union was boycotting the Security Council and was not able to use its veto. As a result the Security Council supported the USA and called on other member states to provide troops. Soldiers from a number of countries fought in Korea, including Britain, Canada, Australia and New Zealand. However, the bulk of the UN forces were provided by the USA.

SOURCE A

General MacArthur, 1949. This US general played a key role in shaping American policy during the Korean War.

The US counter-attack

At first the North Korean attack was very successful. Within four days the Southern capital of Seoul had been captured. The North Koreans conquered all of the country except for a small area in the south around the town of Pusan. In July 1950 MacArthur sent American forces to Pusan and prepared for a counter-attack. The US fight-back began in September. MacArthur organised a successful amphibious attack on the town of Inchon. At the same time US forces broke out of the Pusan area. The counter-attack went extremely well and by 1 October the US troops had reached the 38th parallel, the original border between North and South Korea.

The Americans faced a dilemma. Should they push on and invade North Korea? They now had a chance to go beyond containment and 'roll back' the frontiers of communism. On the other hand, there was a possibility that by invading the North the Americans might provoke China to join the war. MacArthur was keen to go on. Truman approved the change of policy and the US forces crossed the 38th parallel on 7 October. Eventually MacArthur's troops reached the Yalu River, close to the Chinese border. This was the first time since 1945 that Americans had tried to liberate a communist state.

The risk of Chinese intervention

Communist China was a new force in the world. Few people believed that they would risk war with the mighty USA. In early October the Chinese issued a statement that said, 'China will not sit back with folded hands and let the Americans come to the border'. The Americans ignored this warning and continued to march north. On 10 October the Chinese government said that Chinese troops would attack the Americans if MacArthur continued. MacArthur ignored this threat.

SOURCE B

The American view of the dangers of outside help for North Korea was expressed in American magazines of the time.

The danger of Chinese or Soviet intervention if the North Korean Communists are pushed hard to the border is negligible.

Life Magazine, October 1950

If the Chinese should commit their own forces to the struggle in Korea they would do so knowing that they were inviting a general war. That is a price they are not prepared to pay.

The Nation, September 1950

SOURCE C

The communist view was expressed in a Chinese newspaper.

We cannot stand idly by when the American imperialist, a notorious enemy, is now expanding its war of aggression against our neighbour and is attempting to expand the aggressive flames to the borders of our country.

Kung Jen Jih Pao, 13 October 1950

The Chinese intervene

At the end of October Chinese troops went into action and attacked South Korean and American troops. In November the South Koreans and Americans were forced to retreat. Truman and MacArthur were not put off by the Chinese intervention. Britain and France wanted Truman to talk to the Chinese. The advice from these allies was ignored. Instead, MacArthur planned a further push towards the Chinese border. This renewed attack began on 25 November. It went badly wrong. MacArthur made a big mistake: he divided his forces in two and marched north. The Chinese had little difficulty in attacking and destroying many of the US forces. MacArthur had to retreat and the Chinese soon took control of almost all North Korea. Once again it was the turn of the communist forces to push over the border into South Korea. The Chinese offensive continued into the New Year. On 1 January they crossed the 38th parallel, and on 4th January they took the Southern capital, Seoul.

SOURCE D

MacArthur's mistake and retreat was a great blow to the Americans.

There is no doubt that confidence in General MacArthur has been shaken badly as a result of the events of the last few days. Similarly, there is no doubt that the United States leadership in the Western world has been damaged by President Truman's acceptance of the bold MacArthur offensive.

The *New York Times*, 30 November 1950

The success of the Chinese caused great disappointment in America. There were behind-the-scenes arguments about what to do next. General MacArthur recommended extreme action. Truman hinted at a press conference that he might drop the atomic bomb on China.

MACARTHUR'S ADVICE: DECEMBER 1950

> The US should consider all methods to defeat the Chinese; this could include the use of atomic bombs against China.

> The war should be extended to the Chinese mainland in order to cut off supplies to the communist forces in Korea.

> The ultimate aim of the war should be not only the re-capture of North Korea, but also the defeat of communism in China.

The British government was appalled by talk of using atom bombs and invading China. The British Prime Minister, Attlee, flew to Washington and urged Truman to negotiate with the Chinese. Attlee failed to get the Americans to talk to the Chinese but Truman did stop talking about dropping the atom bomb.

SOURCE E

American troops pass through a burning village during the Korean War.

The fall of MacArthur

In February 1951 the Americans launched a further attack on the communist troops. By March the communist forces had been pushed back to the original border, the 38th parallel. At this point MacArthur disagreed with Truman. Truman now abandoned the idea of conquering all of Korea and was considering making peace with China. For a long time there had been tension between Truman and MacArthur. This now reached breaking point. On 24 March MacArthur made a public statement criticising the idea of a deal with the Chinese. Truman was annoyed when he heard this. MacArthur wanted to cross the border again in order to re-conquer North Korea. He sent a message to an American politician explaining his view that America should keep fighting until the Chinese were defeated. Truman was very angry that a general was trying to control the war, instead of obeying his orders, and in April MacArthur was dismissed. This caused a sensation in the United States.

The stalemate

By early summer 1951 the two sides in the Korean War had reached a stalemate. The Chinese launched a huge push south in April and May, but it was not successful. The loss of life on the Chinese side was enormous. In these two months over 200,000 men were killed. Peace talks began in July 1951 but there was no agreed cease-fire. Sporadic but bloody fighting continued. The negotiations soon got stuck over where to draw the border and the exchange of prisoners. As the months passed the situation became similar to the Western Front in the First World War, with both sides dug in to strong defensive positions. This situation continued throughout the second half of 1951 and through the whole of 1952. Soldiers continued to be killed in large numbers on both sides. Between the start of the talks and November 1952, 45,000 American troops were killed or wounded. At the end of 1952 the Americans elected a new President, Ike Eisenhower. The new President took power in January 1953 and he was determined to end the war. An agreement to stop fighting was eventually signed on 27 July 1953.

>> Activity

1 Explain what happened in each of the following phases of the Korean War. For every phase decide whether you think the communists or the anti-communists were more successful.

June 1950 – July 1950

September 1950 – October 1950

November 1950 – January 1951

February 1951 – March 1951

April 1951 – May 1951

July 1951 – July 1953

2 Using all the information in this unit decide whether you think American policy in Korea was successful. Give reasons for your decision.

SOURCE F

Eisenhower. He came to power determined to end the Korean War.

The Cuban missile crisis

Cuba is a large island in the Caribbean. In 1959 a revolution took place in Cuba and Fidel Castro came to power. He introduced a Soviet-style government on the island and he looked to the Soviet Union for support. There was a great uproar in 1962 when the Soviet leader, Khrushchev, placed nuclear missiles on the island.

What happened during the Cuban missile crisis?

The revolution in Cuba was a great blow to America. A communist state had been set up only 90 miles from the USA. In April 1961 the American CIA organised an attack on Cuba. This was carried out by Cuban exiles. Their plan was to land in a remote part of the island and set up a base for guerrilla war against the government of Cuba. They expected that other Cubans would rise up and join the rebellion. The invasion force landed at a place called the Bay of Pigs.

The attack at the Bay of Pigs went disastrously wrong: the Americans had underestimated the strength of the Cuban armed forces and the CIA had misunderstood how popular Castro was. The invasion force was easily defeated by the Cuban government and there was no widespread support for the invasion from among the people of Cuba. The fiasco at the Bay of Pigs was humiliating for the American President, Kennedy.

The struggle for control of Cuba was part of the world-wide Cold War. In early 1962 the Americans placed a number of nuclear missiles in Turkey, within easy range of many cities of the USSR. Shortly afterwards Khrushchev decided to place missiles on Cuba.

THE CUBAN CRISIS, 1962

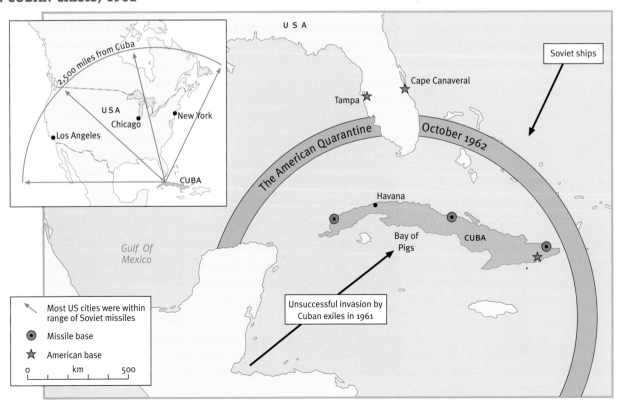

What can we learn from these sources about why Khrushchev placed the missiles on Cuba?

SOURCE A

Khrushchev speaking in December 1962 to the Supreme Soviet (the parliament of the USSR):

Comrades, everyone still remembers the tense days of October when mankind was anxiously listening to the news coming from the Caribbean. In those days the world was on the brink of a nuclear catastrophe. What created this crisis? The revolution in Cuba was met with hostility from the imperialists in the United States of America. The imperialists are frightened of Cuba because of her ideas. They hate the idea that little Cuba has dared go her own way, instead of trying to please American business. American forces have been doing everything they can, from the first day of the revolution, to overthrow Cuba's government and restore their own control. They set up an economic blockade of Cuba. This is inhuman – an attempt to starve a whole nation. Even this was not enough for them. They decided to use force to suppress the Cuban revolution.

We carried weapons there at the request of the Cuban government. Cuba needed weapons as a means of deterring the aggressors, and not as a means of attack. We sent about forty missiles to Cuba. Naturally, neither we nor our Cuban friends thought that this small number of missiles would be used for an attack on the United States. Our aim was only to defend Cuba.

SOURCE B

Fyodor Burlatsky, Khrushchev's assistant, writing in 1992, recalled how the Soviet leader decided to send missiles to Cuba during a visit to Bulgaria in May 1962:

Khrushchev was walking along a beach on the Black Sea with Defence Minister Malinovskiy, who pointed out to him that American military bases with nuclear warheads capable of wiping out the cities of Kiev, Minsk and Moscow in a matter of minutes were located on the opposite shore in Turkey. Khrushchev then asked Malinovskiy, 'And why then can we not have bases close to America? What's the reason for this imbalance?' And right then and there Khrushchev began to question Malinovskiy about whether or not it would be possible to deploy missiles secretly in Cuba. Malinovskiy assured him that the missiles could be deployed without detection.

The crisis

The Soviets tried to move the missiles secretly to the Caribbean. In public Khrushchev stated that 'no missile capable of reaching the United States will be placed in Cuba'. A U-2 spy plane flew over Cuba on 14 October and took photographs of the missile site. On 16 October 1962 President Kennedy was shown the photographs proving that Soviet missiles were on Cuba. The missiles had only recently arrived and would not yet have been in working order. The Americans spent six days secretly discussing and planning how to respond. They did not consult with their allies at this stage. Even the government of Britain, the closest ally, was not told about the missiles until 21 October, shortly before Kennedy made an announcement to the American people.

>> Activity

The Americans considered a range of options:

> a letter of protest to Khrushchev
> bombing the missile sites
> an invasion of Cuba
> a naval blockade of the island.

Imagine that you are Kennedy's adviser. Which of these options would you recommend? Remember you would want to show Khrushchev that you mean business, but you do not want to provoke all-out war with the USSR.

On the edge of a nuclear catastrophe

SOURCE C

MISSILE TRANSPORTERS

12 PROB GUIDELINE MISSILES

HEAVY EQUIPMENT

5 MISSILE DOLLIES

20' LONG CYLINDRICAL TANKS

MISSILE TRANSPORTERS

OPEN STORAGE

Some of the Cuban missile sites, photographed by an American U-2 spy plane.

Kennedy's response to the news of the missiles was twofold: he decided to get ready for an invasion of Cuba, but first of all to mount a blockade of the island. On 22 October a so-called 'quarantine' was announced – the Americans stated that they would stop and search all ships bound for Cuba. Even at this stage, Khrushchev refused to accept publicly that there were missiles on Cuba. This put the USSR in a difficult position when Kennedy was able to show the world that Khrushchev was lying. Two days later a number of Soviet ships, which probably contained warheads for the missiles, turned back just short of the line of the blockade. This was not the end of the crisis because some warheads were already on the island.

The Americans announced that the missiles must be dismantled immediately or else Cuba would be attacked and invaded. There was a real possibility of a nuclear war breaking out between the USA and the USSR. According to one source, Castro actually suggested to Khrushchev that the USSR should launch nuclear missiles against America to stop the imminent invasion of Cuba. Khrushchev was not impressed by this advice and was horrified to discover that some of his top generals thought it would be better to have a nuclear war than back down. Instead he decided to write an urgent letter to Kennedy. This was sent on 26 October.

SOURCE D

On 26 October Khrushchev sent a letter to Kennedy. It suggested that the missiles could be withdrawn if the USA made a promise not to invade Cuba.

If the assurances were given that the President of the United States would not participate in an attack on Cuba and the blockade lifted, then the question of the removal of the missile sites would be an entirely different question. This is my proposal. No more weapons to Cuba and those within Cuba withdrawn or destroyed, and you reciprocate by ending your blockade and also agree not to invade Cuba.

Before Kennedy had replied to this message Khrushchev sent a second letter on 27 October, with different demands. This second letter demanded that the Americans must take their missiles out of Turkey in return for the removal of the Cuban missiles.

SOURCE E

This an extract from Khrushchev's letter of 27 October.

You are worried over Cuba. You say that it worries you because it lies ninety miles across the sea from the shores of the United States. However, Turkey lies next to us. You have stationed devastating rocket weapons in Turkey, literally right next to us. This is why I make this proposal: We agree to remove the weapons from Cuba. We agree to this and to state this commitment in the United Nations. Your representatives will make a statement that the United States, on its part, will evacuate its similar weapons from Turkey.

The Americans did not know how to respond. The Americans had already considered taking their missiles out of Turkey but Kennedy did not want to be seen to be backing down in the face of Soviet pressure. The American military leaders recommended an immediate air attack on Cuba. Kennedy was unsure. A letter was about to be sent to Khrushchev refusing to do a deal over the Turkish missiles. At this point it was suggested that the Americans ignore the second letter, but reply to the first letter accepting the Soviet proposal that the missiles should be withdrawn in return for an American commitment not to invade Cuba. The President liked this idea and a suitable letter was sent.

The President's brother

Later on the 27 October Robert Kennedy, the brother of the President, went to see the Soviet ambassador. The conversation between Robert Kennedy and the ambassador, Anatoly Dobrynin, was the key to the solution of the crisis. Kennedy gave Dobrynin an ultimatum; he said that if the Soviets did not promise to remove the missiles by the next day the Americans would use force to destroy the missiles. He then made an offer to the Russians – there could be no official deal, but if the Cuban missiles were removed the missiles in Turkey would follow soon after. This message was relayed to Khrushchev, and it was enough for the Russians. On 28 October Dobrynin reported to back to Robert Kennedy and announced that the Russians would withdraw their missiles from Cuba. The crisis was over.

SOURCE F

A few years later, in 1969, Robert Kennedy's account of his crucial conversation with Dobrynin was published.

I said that there could be no arrangement made under this kind of threat or pressure. However, I said that President Kennedy had been anxious to remove those missiles from Turkey and Italy for a long period of time. It was our judgement that, within a short time after this crisis was over, those missiles would be gone.

SOURCE G

Robert Kennedy. The President's brother finally negotiated an end to the crisis with the Soviet ambassador to Washington.

SOURCE I

AFTER THE CRISIS

> The end of the crisis was seen as a victory for Kennedy and a defeat for Khrushchev. The deal over the missiles in Turkey was kept secret so it seemed to the world as if the Soviets had simply backed down. This was good for Kennedy's reputation, but damaging for the Soviet leader. Leading Soviet communists were angry that their country appeared to climb down. This put Khrushchev in a difficult position at home, and contributed to his fall from power in 1964.

> The European allies of the USA were shocked at how little they were consulted during the emergency. It seemed that their opinions was not seen as important by the Americans. The French government of de Gaulle felt this very strongly. As a result de Gaulle eventually pulled France out of NATO and encouraged Western Europe to follow an independent line.

> On the communist side, the Chinese were not impressed by the Soviet performance. They felt that Khrushchev mishandled the crisis and looked cowardly when he removed the missiles. This further encouraged the Chinese to follow an independent line of their own in world politics.

Nikita Khrushchev.

> The most important long-term result of the crisis was that both sides realised the great dangers of direct conflict between the USSR and the USA. Both Soviet and American leaders were shocked at how close they had come to nuclear war. After the Cuban Missile Crisis the Cold War continued but the two superpowers carefully avoided direct hostility. A special telephone 'hotline' was installed so that leaders could communicate easily in any future crisis. The level of tension between the USA and the USSR was never again to be as great as it was in November 1962.

SOURCE H

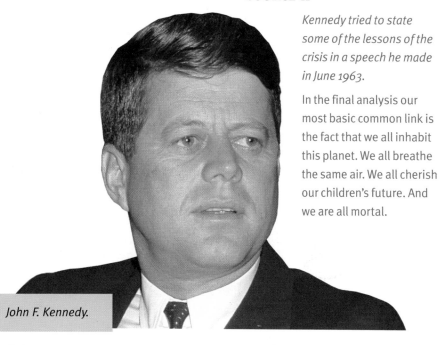

John F. Kennedy.

Kennedy tried to state some of the lessons of the crisis in a speech he made in June 1963.

In the final analysis our most basic common link is the fact that we all inhabit this planet. We all breathe the same air. We all cherish our children's future. And we are all mortal.

>> **Activity**

Explain in your own words how the crisis:

a appeared to be a victory for Kennedy and a defeat for Khrushchev,

b damaged the relationship between the superpowers and other states,

c led to a period of greater stability in Soviet–US relations.

The Cold War and the Middle East

Israel and the superpowers

Throughout much of the twentieth century there was a bitter argument between Jewish and Arab people over control of the area of the Middle East originally known as Palestine. Until the First World War the territory was part of the Turkish Empire. It was then controlled by the British. After the Second World War the United Nations decided to set up a Jewish state, called Israel, in part of Palestine. As British forces left the area in May 1948, Jewish leaders declared the existence of the new state. Israel was immediately attacked by the neighbouring Arab states of Egypt, Jordan, Syria, Lebanon and Iraq. Fighting came to an end in January 1949 with Israel victorious but this was not the end of the dispute. The two superpowers soon took sides in this conflict. Israel became strongly pro-American, while the Soviet Union became hostile towards Israel.

Suez

There was an upsurge of Arab nationalism in the 1950s supported by the Soviet Union. In 1952 a passionate Arab nationalist called Gamal Nasser took power in Egypt. He turned to the Soviet Union for help in developing the country. In 1956 Nasser seized control of the Suez Canal from the Western powers of Britain and France.

In October 1956 Britain, France and Israel attacked the Suez Canal area. The government of the USA was unhappy about the invasion of Egypt and forced Britain and France to pull out. The Americans got little credit for their actions and radical Arabs increasingly looked to the USSR for assistance. After Suez there was increased Soviet involvement in the Middle East.

War and peace

War broke out again between Israel and the Arab states in 1967 and in 1973. Israel won both these wars and gained control of substantial lands inhabited by Palestinian Arabs. The success of Israel was a blow to the USSR. The Soviets had supplied Egypt and Syria with their weapons but they had lost. Israel was a small country but, with

American help, the Israelis had defeated their hostile neighbours. After 1973 the USA was much more successful than the USSR in influencing events in the Middle East. A new Egyptian leader, Anwar Sadat, broke off relations with the Soviet Union and established a good relationship with the USA. With American help and encouragement the states of Egypt and Israel signed a peace treaty in 1979. In the 1980s the Americans tried to bring Jewish Israelis and Arab Palestinians together. After many years of American pressure the Palestinian leader, Yasser Arafat, signed a peace treaty with the Israeli Prime Minister, Yitzhak Rabin, in 1993. By this time the Soviet Union had fallen apart and the Soviet leaders did not play a significant part in the Middle East peace treaty.

US President Clinton encourages Yitzhak Rabin and Yasser Arafat to shake hands in Washington in 1993.

Discussion points

> Which superpower was more successful in influencing Middle East politics?

The Vietnam War

Between 1965 and 1973 US troops fought a disastrous war against communists in South Vietnam. In the end, the wealthiest country in the world was unable to defeat the Vietnamese fighters.

Why did the USA fight and lose the Vietnam War?

Vietnam divided

Vietnam had been a French colony. After the Second World War, Vietnamese nationalists and communists, led by Ho Chi Minh, fought against the French. In 1954 the French decided to pull out and Vietnam was divided in two. Communists took power in North Vietnam. South Vietnam was ruled by an anti-communist leader called Ngo Dinh Diem. In 1959 the communist government of the North decided to encourage a revolution in the South. Southern communists, who had fled North, returned to fight. These forces were known as the Vietcong.

From 1954 South Vietnam depended on aid from the USA. American policy was based on the 'domino theory': the belief that, because neighbouring states are so interdependent, the collapse of one will lead to the collapse of others. The Americans used this theory as a justification of their involvement in foreign states, particularly in South-East Asia, which they felt were likely to be taken over by the communists. In November 1961 President Kennedy began providing wide-ranging support for the army of the South, including some American soldiers as 'combat advisers'. He hoped that with this help Diem would be able to defeat the communist rebels. This did not happen. The Americans became increasingly unhappy with Diem. In 1963 Diem's government further annoyed the USA by clashing with local Buddhists. With American approval, a group of South Vietnamese generals overthrew Diem in a coup in November 1963.

The Gulf of Tonkin Incident

In 1964 regular North Vietnamese forces marched south along what became known as the Ho Chi Minh Trail to support the Vietcong. Without outside help South Vietnam looked doomed. American involvement increased dramatically after a clash at sea between North Vietnam and the USA in August 1964. An American destroyer near the coast of North Vietnam was attacked by North Vietnamese ships. No serious damage was done in this so-called Gulf of Tonkin Incident. However, the new American President, Johnson, ordered the bombing of Northern naval bases in retaliation. Congress passed a resolution giving the President power to 'take all necessary steps, including the use of armed force' in order to defend South Vietnam. After this Johnson felt he had full authority to step up American involvement in the war.

THE VIETNAM WAR

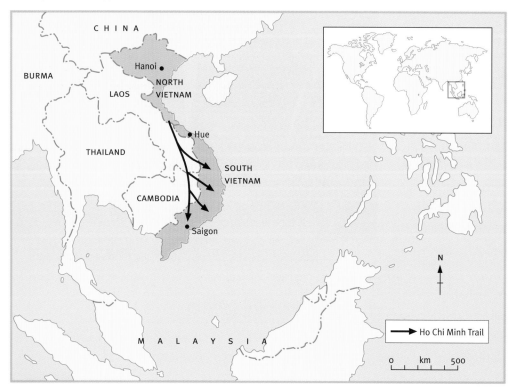

The arrival of US ground troops

By early 1965 American bombers were regularly attacking targets in the North. Johnson did not think that this was enough. He decided that the South Vietnamese needed the help of large numbers of American soldiers on the ground. In July 1965 President Johnson took a fateful step: he agreed to send 180,000 American troops to Vietnam. The number of US troops increased over the next three years until there were 540,000 American soldiers in Vietnam.

SOURCE A

An American B-52 bomber attacks a target near Hanoi, 1966. The US tried to use its massive firepower to force the communists to retreat.

>> Activity

What can you learn from Sources B–D about why the USA got involved in Vietnam?

SOURCE B

Robert McNamara, US Secretary of Defense, March 1964:

We seek an independent, non-communist South Vietnam. Unless we can achieve this objective in South Vietnam, almost all of South-East Asia will probably fall under Communist dominance. Thailand might hold for a period with our help, but would be under grave pressure. Even the Philippines would become shaky, and the threat to India to the west, Australia and New Zealand to the south, and Taiwan, Korea and Japan to the north and east would be greatly increased.

SOURCE C

President Johnson, August 1964:

The challenge that we face in South-East Asia today is the same challenge that we have faced with courage and that we have met with strength in Greece and Turkey, in Berlin, Korea and in Cuba.

SOURCE D

The US government State Department reviewed its policy on Vietnam in February 1965.

South Vietnam is fighting for its life against a brutal campaign of terror and armed attack directed by the Communist regime in Hanoi. This aggression has been going on for years, but recently the pace has quickened and the threat has now become acute. The war in Vietnam is a new kind of war. A totally new kind of aggression has been loosed against an independent people who want to make their own way in peace and freedom. The war in Vietnam is not a spontaneous and local rebellion against the established Government. In Vietnam, a Communist Government has set out deliberately to conquer a neighbouring state.

The people of South Vietnam have chosen to resist this threat. At their request, the United States has taken its place beside them in their defensive struggle. The United States seeks no territory, no military bases, no favoured position. But we have learned the meaning of aggression elsewhere in the post-war world and we have met it. The United States will not abandon friends who want to remain free. It will do what must be done to help them.

The fighting intensifies

The arrival of large numbers of American soldiers stopped the collapse of South Vietnam and strengthened the position of the new South Vietnamese leader, General Thieu. Between 1965 and 1967 there was heavy fighting. The Americans regularly bombed North Vietnam. According to one calculation, more bombs were dropped on North Vietnam than on Germany in the Second World War. American involvement was widely criticised, and many people in the USA were unhappy about the war.

American tactics brought little success. The US forces had the technology to win straightforward battles between tanks or massed infantry. However, the Vietcong and the soldiers of North Vietnam refused to fight this kind of war. Instead they relied on guerrilla tactics: sabotage and sudden ambushes. The American response was to use:

> massive airpower to try to bomb supply lines,

> chemical defoliants to destroy areas of the countryside where communist soldiers might be hiding.

Neither of these methods worked; they simply angered the ordinary people of the Vietnamese countryside and increased support for the Vietcong and Ho Chi Minh.

The Tet Offensive

In January 1968 North Vietnam launched a massive attack at the time of Tet, a religious festival. Communist troops attacked towns all over the country. They struck right in the middle of the Southern capital of Saigon, with attacks on the American embassy. The communists hoped that the Tet Offensive would spark a popular revolution in the South. This did not happen. The losses on the communist side were enormous. About 50,000 communist troops were killed between January and March. The Americans used great force and won back the towns. American guns destroyed the historic centre of the ancient city of Hue, killing many civilians.

What were the results of the Tet Offensive?

The Tet Offensive was a turning-point in the war. Although in the short term it was a failure for the communists, in the long run it helped the North to win the war. The sight of communist fighters in the grounds of the American embassy in Saigon made a mockery of the idea that Americans were close to victory. As a result of the violence of the attack and the clear determination of the communists, many American politicians and people became disillusioned with the war. The anti-war movement in the USA grew in strength. Leading figures in the government began to think that they could not win the war in Vietnam.

SOURCE E

A Vietcong fighter lies dead in the grounds of the US embassy, Saigon, during the Tet Offensive, 1968. This was a turning-point in the war.

>> Activity

Look at the following quotations from the American adviser, Dean Acheson, made before and after the Tet Offensive. What difference is there between the two statements?

SOURCE F

Dean Acheson in November 1967:

We can and will win. We must not have negotiations. When these fellows decide that they can't defeat the South, then they will give up. This is the way it was in Korea. This is the way the Communists operate.

SOURCE G

Dean Acheson in March 1968:

Neither the effort of the Government of South Vietnam nor the effort of the US government can succeed. Time is limited by reactions in this country. We cannot build an independent South Vietnam. The issue is: can we by military means keep the North Vietnamese off the South Vietnamese? I do not think we can.

Johnson bows out and peace talks begin

At the end of March 1968 Johnson admitted that he had failed in Vietnam. Presidential elections were due later in the year; Johnson declared that he would not be seeking re-election. He reduced the level of bombing in the North. He called for peace talks. North Vietnam agreed to negotiate and talks began in Paris in May 1968.

The peace talks got nowhere, but it was clear by the summer of 1968 that the American government was looking for a way out. A new President was elected in November 1968 – Richard Nixon – and he was determined to end the war.

Nixon searches for peace with honour

The challenge for Nixon was to find a way out of Vietnam without humiliation or the clear abandoning of South Vietnam. Nixon tried a number of methods:

1. At the Paris peace talks he tried to persuade North Vietnam that North Vietnamese soldiers should withdraw from the South at the same time as American troops. He threatened a massive attack on the North if they refused to compromise. Nixon was bluffing, and the government of North Vietnam called his bluff. They refused to make a deal but Nixon did not launch an attack.

2. Nixon tried to persuade the USSR and China to use their influence over the government of the North. He told the Soviets and the Chinese that if they helped him over Vietnam the Americans would help them in other areas. This approach did not work. The USSR and China saw no reason to try to help the Americans over Vietnam.

3. Nixon decided to put more of the burden of the war on the shoulders of the government of South Vietnam. He reduced the number of American soldiers and insisted that more of the fighting should be done by South Vietnamese. In April 1969 there were 543,000 American troops in Vietnam. By 1971 the number had gone down to 157,000. This policy of passing responsibility to South Vietnam was known as 'Vietnamisation'.

SOURCE H

A British cartoonist, Nicholas Garland, ridicules Nixon's policy in 1969.
> What point is the cartoonist trying to make?

Atrocities at My Lai

The American war effort was hit by another devastating blow in 1969. It became known that US troops had carried out an appalling atrocity against Vietnamese civilians. On 16 March 1968 American soldiers massacred the villagers of a place called My Lai. The American officer, Lieutenant William Calley, was eventually court-martialled for the murder of 109 civilians. The story of what happened at My Lai horrified many Americans. They had seen their action in Vietnam as a fight against wicked communists. In My Lai all the wickedness was American.

SOURCE J

Murdered women and children at My Lai, 1968.

SOURCE I

In 1969 Time Magazine *reported a series of interviews with American soldiers who had fought at My Lai.*

Varnado Simpson: 'Everyone who went into the village had in mind to kill. We had lost a lot of buddies and the village was a VC [Vietcong] stronghold. We considered them either VC or helping the VC. As I came up on the village there was a woman, a man and a child running away. I told them in their language to stop. They didn't, and I had orders to shoot them down and I did this. This is what I did. I shot them: the lady and the little boy. He was about two years old.

Jay Roberts: 'Just outside the village there was this big pile of bodies. This really tiny kid – he had only a shirt on, nothing else – he came over to the pile and held the hand of one of the dead. One of the GIs behind me dropped into a kneeling position thirty metres from this kid and killed him with a single shot.'

Paul Meadlo: 'We ran through My Lai herding men, women, children and babies into the centre of the village. Lieutenant Calley came over and said, "You know what to do with them, don't you?" And I said, "Yes." and he left and came back about ten minutes later, and said, "How come you ain't killed them yet?" And I told him that I didn't think he wanted us to kill them, just to guard them. He said, "No, I want them dead." So he started shooting them. And he told me to start shooting. I might have killed ten or fifteen of them.'

Protests against the war

News of the atrocities at My Lai fuelled the anti-war feelings of many Americans. The war was shown on American television and this also caused many people to question why their country was fighting in Vietnam. As the peace talks made little progress in Paris there were increasing numbers of demonstrations in America calling for an end to the war.

SOURCE K

The British journalist, John Pilger, described the scene on 25 April 1971 when a huge demonstration of veterans, or former soldiers, protested in Washington against the war.

'The truth is out! Mickey Mouse is dead! The good guys are really the bad guys in disguise!' The speaker is William Wyman, from New York City. He is nineteen and has no legs. He sits in a wheelchair on the steps of the United States Congress, in the midst of 300,000, the greatest demonstration America has ever seen. He has on green combat fatigues and the jacket is torn where he has ripped away the medals and the ribbons he has been given in exchange for his legs.

Along with hundreds of other veterans of the war, he has hurled his medals on the Capitol steps and described them as shit. And now to those who form a ring of pity around him, he says, 'Before I lost these legs, I killed and killed and killed! We all did! Jesus, don't grieve for me!'

Never before in this country have young soldiers marched in protest against the war in which they themselves have fought and which is still going on.

Did Vietnamisation work?

The South Vietnamese forces were not strong enough to defeat the communists. The government of General Thieu lacked the support and loyalty of the Vietnamese people. Thieu had the backing of landlords and Catholic Church leaders but crucially he had little support from the ordinary Vietnamese people in the countryside.

SOURCE M

When Nixon later wrote his memoirs he recognised the weakness of Vietnamisation.

The real problem was that the enemy was willing to sacrifice in order to win, while the South Vietnamese simply weren't willing to pay that much of a price in order to avoid losing.

As part of Vietnamisation the USA stepped up the bombing of the supply lines of the Viet Cong. This had the effect of spreading the conflict into neighbouring countries of Laos and Cambodia. The attacks on these countries did little to stop the supplies to the communist troops but did manage to encourage local communists. Between 1969 and 1973 the US dropped over half a million tons of bombs on Cambodia. This contributed to the support for the ruthless Cambodian communists, known as the Khmer Rouge. Communists won control of Cambodia in 1975. Similarly, the communist force known as Pathet Lao gained support in Laos and took control of the whole country in 1975.

I WANT OUT

An American anti-war poster. It shows Uncle Sam as a wounded veteran who has had enough of the war. It is a parody of a First World War recruitment poster.

SOURCE L

The cease-fire: 1973

The peace talks in Paris dragged on for years without achieving anything. By 1972 the communists felt strong enough to launch another all-out attack on the cities of the South, similar to the Tet Offensive. This attack was more successful than the Tet Offensive but the communists were still not able to conquer the main centres of population. After the offensive of the summer of 1972, neither side could see any hope of victory and the peace talks started to make some progress. At last in January 1973 a cease-fire was agreed and the Americans started to take their troops home.

The fall of the South: 1975

The American forces pulled out soon after the cease-fire agreement was signed. This ended US involvement but it did not end the war. Fighting soon resumed between the communists and the Southern forces. Two years after the agreement in Paris the North launched another major offensive against South Vietnam in March 1975. This time, relying only on South Vietnamese troops and without American air support, the Saigon government was not able to resist. The Vietcong and the army of the North swept victoriously through the South. The war effectively ended on 29 April 1975 when the communists captured the southern capital of Saigon. American TV viewers watched in horror as thousands of south Vietnamese people fought to get on the last US helicopters out of Saigon.

After Vietnam: détente and a loss of confidence

American failure to contain communism in Vietnam led to a deep re-assessment of policy towards the communist world. American leaders had been shocked by their failure in Vietnam. The cost had been enormous: 55,000 dead American soldiers and billions of dollars spent. This huge commitment had achieved nothing. Communist governments had taken power not only in North and South Vietnam but also in the neighbouring states of Cambodia and Laos. In addition, Americans had lost the confidence in their mission as the world's leading nation.

The American President who took the US out of the war was Richard Nixon. Together with his adviser, Henry Kissinger, Nixon developed a new foreign policy for the post-Vietnam world. This became known as 'détente' and it involved striving for agreement and peace with the communist world.

>> Activity

Explain why the USA lost the war in Vietnam. In your answer describe:

a American military tactics,

b the impact of the Tet Offensive,

c atrocities such as My Lai,

d opposition to the war in the USA.

SOURCE N

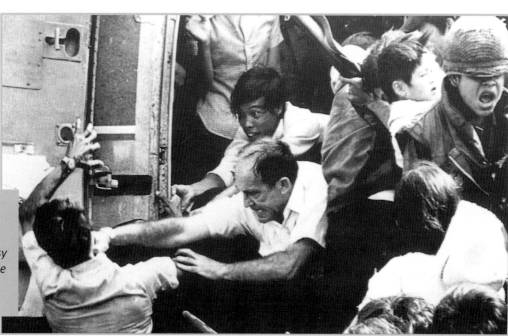

Desperate scenes as the last US helicopters leave Saigon, just before the communist victory in 1975. A US embassy official punches a Vietnamese man who is trying to board the helicopter.

Nixon in China

Nixon tried to get better relations not only with the Soviet Union, but also with communist China. The world was surprised when Nixon announced in 1971 that he would visit China. Since 1949 the US government had treated China with contempt and had refused to 'recognise' the communist government. The visit took place in 1972 and led to much better relations between the two countries.

SOURCE O

The world was astonished when Nixon visited China in 1972.

Arms control

In dealing with the Soviet Union, Nixon emphasised the need for arms control negotiations. The Strategic Arms Limitation Talks (SALT 1) began in 1969 and led to the signing of an agreement on Intercontinental Ballistic Missiles in 1972. Nixon stated that American policy on nuclear weapons was now one of 'sufficiency', rather than 'superiority': this meant that the Americans wanted enough weapons to defend themselves and were no longer committed to having more than the Soviet Union. Détente also increased trade between the superpowers. In 1972 the US government agreed to supply wheat to the Soviet Union and soon a large proportion of all American wheat was exported to the Soviet Union.

In Europe, détente meant a reduction of tension over the divisions of Germany. In 1974 the USA formally recognised East Germany as an independent country. Détente allowed the two German states to establish better relations with each other.

Détente continued after Nixon's fall from office during the Watergate Scandal in 1974. Brezhnev, the Soviet leader organised a conference on the future of Europe in Helsinki between 1973 and 1975. This produced agreements on ways of avoiding confrontation between East and West and economic co-operation. The Helsinki agreements also committed all parties to respect human rights. Communist countries did very little to honour the pledge on human rights.

The end of détente

The US president, Jimmy Carter (in office 1977–80) attempted to achieve more arms reductions through the SALT 2 talks. These talks were very protracted. Carter annoyed Brezhnev by trying to link cuts in weapons to discussions of human rights in the communist countries. A SALT 2 treaty was finally signed in 1979. This set further limits on the number of nuclear weapons that each side could hold. The SALT 2 treaty was never ratified by the US Congress because the Soviet Union invaded Afghanistan in December 1979. The sending of troops into Afghanistan marked the end of the period of détente. The USA boycotted the Moscow Olympics in 1980 in order to show disapproval for the Soviet nation. In 1981, Carter was replaced by a hard-line President, Ronald Reagan, who rejected détente and who started a new arms race with the Soviet Union. The early 1980s have been called the Second Cold War. Reagan attacked Soviet communism in his speeches and talked of the need to oppose an 'evil empire'. His scientists were instructed to explore ways of giving the USA nuclear superiority by developing ways of shooting down Soviet missiles in space. This project was known as Star Wars, or the Strategic Defence Initiative.

>> Activity

Explain in your own words how American foreign policy developed after Vietnam.

Containing communism

After the communist take-over of Eastern Europe, US governments were preoccupied with the need to stop the spread of communism. This policy was called containment.

The fall of China: 1949

Led by Mao Zedong, communists took power in China in 1949. Communist success in China convinced American leaders that they needed to be more energetic in a worldwide struggle against communism. This led to a huge increase in American spending on defence.

The Korean War: 1950–3

At the end of the Second World War, Korea was divided in two at the 38th parallel – North Korea was communist, South Korea was anti-communist. North Korea invaded South Korea in June 1950. The Americans won UN support for a war against the invading North Koreans. General MacArthur led a fight-back that drove the North Koreans out of South Korea. MacArthur then continued to push deep into North Korean territory. This was going beyond 'containment' and became an attempt to 'roll back' communism.

A massive Chinese army invaded to help the North Koreans in November 1950. The US army was driven back close to the original border in early 1951. There was then a military stalemate. MacArthur wanted to widen the war by attacking China itself. President Truman disagreed and dismissed MacArthur. Peace talks dragged on for two years. The war finally ended in July 1953.

The Cuban Missile Crisis: 1962

Led by Fidel Castro, there was a revolution in Cuba in 1959. Castro introduced communist ideas to Cuba. The US attempted to invade and overthrow Castro, but this ended in disaster at the Bay of Pigs in 1961.

In 1962 Khrushchev, the Soviet leader, placed nuclear missiles on Cuba. American spy planes discovered them and the American President, Kennedy, insisted that the missiles should be removed. There was a real possibility of a nuclear war. Eventually Khrushchev gave way and agreed to remove the missiles in return for a US promise to remove missiles in Turkey. The ending of the crisis was seen as a victory for Kennedy and a defeat for Khrushchev.

Fidel Castro.

Restricting Soviet influence in the Middle East

Both the USA and the Soviet Union tried to influence states in the Middle East. The US encouraged the new Jewish state of Israel, set up in 1948. Some Arabs, including the governments of Egypt and Syria and the Palestine Liberation Organisation (PLO), looked for Soviet help in their conflict with Israel. With American money and weapons, Israel was able to defeat its Arab enemies in a series of wars (1948–9, 1967, 1973). These defeats convinced the Egyptian president, Sadat, to break with the USSR. The US government enabled Israel and Egypt to sign a peace treaty in 1979.

The Vietnam War: 1965–1975

Vietnam had been a French colony before the Second World War. The French pulled out in 1954 and Vietnam was divided between a communist state in the North, and and an anti-communist state in South Vietnam. The leader of North Vietnam was Ho Chi Minh.

After 1958 communist guerillas, known as the Vietcong, helped by troops of the regular army of North Vietnam, tried to overthrow the government of South Vietnam. At first the Americans supplied the South with money and weapons and in March 1965 President Johnson sent US combat troops to Vietnam. Eventually there were 540,000 Americans fighting in Vietnam.

The defeat of the USA

The USA was unable to defeat the Vietcong. Many people in the USA were opposed to the war. In January 1968 the Vietcong launched a massive series of attacks called the Tet Offensive. This was not a military success but it convinced American leaders that they would never win in Vietnam. President Johnson was replaced by Richard Nixon, who was determined to pull out of Vietnam. Nixon tried 'Vietnamisation' – a policy of reducing American troops and trying to strengthen the forces of South Vietnam. In 1973 the US signed a peace treaty with North Vietnam and Americans troops left the country. Vietnamisation did not work – without American forces the government of South Vietnam was overthrown by communist forces in 1975. Vietnam became a single, communist state. After the fall of Vietnam several neighbouring countries also became communist.

After Vietnam: détente

The US presidents of the 1970s – Nixon, Ford and Carter – pursued a policy of 'détente'. This involved establishing peaceful relationships with the two great communist powers: the USSR and China.

Defeat in Vietnam reduced American self-confidence.
Further disasters followed:

> The pro-American government in Iran was overthrown in a revolution in 1978. American diplomats were taken prisoner and were held hostage from 1979–81.

> A Soviet army invaded Afghanistan in 1979 to support its new communist government.

Ho Chi Minh.

The end of détente

The new US President, Ronald Reagan, restored some of America's self-confidence in the 1980s. He ended détente. He aggressively challenged the Soviet Union and began a new arms race. This period has been called the Second Cold War. Reagan invested in 'Star Wars' (officially known as the Strategic Defence Initiative). This was intended to be a system for shooting down Soviet missiles in space. The Soviet Union could not compete. Gorbachev came to power in the Soviet Union and established good relations with Reagan. The arms race came to an end and the Soviet Union pulled out of Afghanistan in 1988–9.

Tito and Stalin

Orders from Moscow

After 1945 communists took power in some countries without Soviet help. This happened in Yugoslavia, where a communist leader called Tito led a successful war against occupying German forces between 1941 and 1945. At first, Tito seemed to be highly regarded by Stalin. In April 1945 Tito went on a tour of the USSR and was treated as a great hero. There was, however, an underlying tension between Tito and Stalin. The Yugoslav leader did not see why he should follow orders from Moscow.

Tito, the Leader of Yugoslavia. He successfully defied Stalin.

Tito and Stalin argued in 1948. There were two immediate causes of this rift between Yugoslavia and the USSR:

> Yugoslav foreign policy was at odds with Soviet plans. Tito wanted to control the small neighbouring state of Albania. In late 1947 the Yugoslavs annoyed Stalin by sending their troops into Albania.

> Tito was greatly offended by the way the Soviets recruited agents in Yugoslavia and asked them to report direct to Moscow. Many senior members of the army were asked to become Soviet spies.

'I will shake my little finger'

The conflict between Stalin and Tito was announced to the world in June 1948. Yugoslavia was thrown out of Cominform, the Soviet-led organisation for world communism. Stalin took action to bring Tito into line. Economic sanctions were used – the USSR and other East European states stopped trading with Yugoslavia. Stalin was confident that Tito could be overthrown. At the beginning of the split he said, 'I will shake my little finger and there will be no more Tito'. Stalin hoped that Yugoslav communists would turn against their leader. Tito dealt skilfully with his enemies. Local communists who sided with Stalin were arrested. People in Yugoslavia rallied round their leader.

Tito turns West

Tito believed that the USA and other Western countries would support him in his dispute with Stalin. He was right. Western countries were keen to help Yugoslavia survive the economic blockade. In December 1948 the British provided a $30 million trade deal. Over the next few years the Americans gave considerable financial support. With Western help Tito survived the early days of the split with Stalin. Having failed through other means Stalin began, in 1949, to threaten war. In the early 1950s the West began to give direct military help, as well as money. In 1951 the Americans provided the Yugoslav armed forces with equipment worth $60 million dollars.

Stalin spent his final years making sure that no other East European leaders tried to follow Tito. Some were accused of 'Titoism' and executed. According to some sources Stalin was making plans to have Tito poisoned when he himself died in 1953. After the death of Stalin, the new Soviet leader, Khrushchev, ended the dispute with Yugoslavia in 1955. This was a victory for Tito, who continued with his independent foreign policy.

Discussion points

> Why did Tito and Stalin argue?

> How successful were Stalin's attempts to destroy Tito?

The Red Army in Budapest and Prague

In 1956 the Soviet Union shocked the world by sending troops to overthrow the government of Hungary. A similar invasion of Czechoslovakia took place in 1968.

Why did the Soviet Union invade Hungary and Czechoslovakia?

>> Activity

Imagine that you were working for the United Nations in 1956. You have been asked to write a report on why the Soviet Union invaded Hungary. In your report you should discuss:

> why Hungarians disliked Soviet rule

> how the death of Stalin created a new situation in Eastern Europe

> the impact on Hungarians of events in Yugoslavia and Poland

> how the Soviet Union reacted to changes in Hungary.

SOURCE A

Cardinal Mindszenty, leader of the Catholic Church in Hungary. As an opponent of Soviet communism he was sentenced to life in prison.

Hungary and the Soviet Empire

The Hungarians were a proud nation with a strong sense of identity. Before 1918 they played a key part in the running of the vast Austro–Hungarian Empire. Hungarian nationalists did not like being part of a Soviet Empire after the Second World War.

Stalin's actions increased anti-Soviet feelings in Hungary. Free elections were held in November 1945. The communists got less than 20 per cent of the vote. Stalin ignored the decision of the Hungarian people and imposed a government on the country in which communists had many of the most important posts. In August 1947 another election was held in Hungary. This time the Soviet Union made sure that the election was rigged so that the communists won. Between 1949 and 1953 Hungary was badly treated by Stalin. Opponents of Soviet power were dealt with ruthlessly. In 1949 the leader of the Roman Catholic Church in Hungary, Cardinal Mindszenty, was sentenced to life imprisonment. Even Hungarian communists were attacked if they showed any signs of disagreeing with Stalin. The leading communist, Laszlo Rajk, was put on trial and hanged in 1949 because he was too independent-minded.

After Stalin

The death of Stalin in 1953 created a new uncertain situation in Eastern Europe. During the Stalinist years, Hungary had been ruled with considerable brutality by Mátyás Rákosi. Rákosi managed to hang on to power after 1953, but he was forced to invite a reformer called Imre Nagy to join his government. The two men got on badly and in 1955 Rákosi got the upper hand and threw Nagy out of the government and the party.

Hungarians were not sure how far the new Soviet leadership would allow Hungary to operate as an independent country. For a number of reasons Hungarians hoped that they might be able to have greater independence:

> The new Soviet leadership was friendly to Tito's Yugoslavia. Yugoslavia had successfully broken away from Soviet control in 1948. People in Hungary thought that other countries could now follow the Yugoslav path.

> Stalin was criticised by the new Soviet leader, Khrushchev, in a famous speech in February 1956. Hungarians hoped that Khrushchev would be very different from Stalin and would be happy with a new, independent Hungary.

> In June 1956 there were anti-Soviet demonstrations in Poland. Khrushchev looked for a compromise. He allowed reforms and he appointed Gomulka, a man who had been imprisoned by Stalin, as the new leader of the Polish Communist Party.

The news from Poland seemed like further proof that the bad old days of Soviet control were over. In fact this was a mistake: the new Soviet leaders still wanted to control the countries of the Warsaw Pact. Hungarians listened to radio broadcasts from the West that criticised communism. Some felt that if Hungary challenged Soviet power they could expect help from the USA. Back in 1948 the Truman Doctrine had stated that the USA would help any people fighting against communism. In practice, the US theory of containment meant that America would only threaten force to stop the spread of communism; countries that were already communist could expect sympathy but no help.

SOURCE B

In 1955 Khrushchev visited Yugoslavia to make friends with Tito. He made a speech claiming that the USSR no longer wished to interfere in other states.

True to the teaching of the founder of the Soviet State, Lenin, the government of the Soviet Union bases its policy towards other countries, big and small, on the principle of peaceful co-existence. We believe in equality, non-interference, respect for sovereignty and national independence. The Soviet Union rejects aggression and believes that any invasion of another state is not to be permitted.

Alarm in Moscow

There was an air of excitement in Hungary in the summer of 1956. People heard the news from Poland. They wanted even more change in Hungary. They talked about Hungary breaking away from the Soviet bloc and becoming a neutral country. This was too much for Khrushchev. He could accept some changes but not Hungarian neutrality. If Hungary left the Warsaw Pact, other countries might follow. The protective buffer of friendly countries built up by Stalin might fall apart.

The Soviet leaders tried to stop the disturbances in Hungary by changing the leadership of the Hungarian communists. Realising that Rákosi was extremely unpopular, the Soviet leadership forced him to resign in July 1956. The new ruler was Ernö Gerö. However, Gerö was seen as a Stalinist by many Hungarians and the change of leader made little difference.

On 6 October 1956, Laszlo Rajk, the leading victim of Stalinist terror, was re-buried with a state funeral. A huge crowd turned out to show their support for the memory of Rajk and the idea of reform. Further demonstrations called for the removal of Gerö and the reinstatement of the popular reformer Nagy. On 24 October Nagy became Prime Minister. Khrushchev had hoped that this would end the disturbances. It did not. Across the country, workers set up revolutionary councils. They demanded a complete end to the Soviet system in Hungary. They called for free multi-party elections, a free Press and for Hungary to leave the Warsaw Pact. Nagy agreed to accept these reforms. At this point Khrushchev decided to invade.

SOURCE C

Laszlo Rajk, on trial for his life. Stalin was afraid that this communist leader would copy Tito and break away from Moscow. Stalin ensured that Rajk was executed.

SOURCE D

The Soviet leader, Khrushchev, expressed his anxiety over Hungary in July 1956.

If the situation in Hungary gets still worse, we here have decided to use all means at our disposal to bring the crisis to an end. The Soviet Union could not at any price allow a breach in the front in Eastern Europe.

SOURCE E

The Soviet Foreign Minister, Shepilov, explained Soviet actions to the General Assembly of the United Nations on 19 November 1956.

We could not overlook the fact that Hungary is a neighbour of the Soviet Union. A victory of the reactionary forces would have converted that country into a new jumping-off ground for an aggressive war not only against the Soviet Union but also against the other countries of Eastern Europe.

>> **Activity**

1 Look at Source B. Why do you think that Hungarians who wished for independence were encouraged by Khrushchev's speech in 1955?

2 Look at the Sources D and E. What do they tell us about Soviet motives in invading Hungary?

The Soviet invasion

The Soviet forces reached Budapest on 4 November 1956. The Red Army forces comprised 200,000 soldiers and 2,500 tanks. The Hungarians fought against the invaders. At least 3,000 Hungarians were killed (some estimates are much higher). Despite Nagy's desperate appeal (Source G) neither the United Nations nor the USA did anything to help. The powerful Soviet forces took control of Hungary and imposed a new pro-Soviet government.

SOURCE F

Hungarian nationalists engaged in street fighting in Budapest, 4 November 1956.

SOURCE G

When he heard of the invasion, Imre Nagy, the Hungarian Prime Minister, appealed to the United Nations for help.

Reliable reports have reached the government of the Hungarian People's Republic that further Soviet units are entering Hungary. The Hungarian government immediately repudiates the Warsaw Treaty and declares Hungary's neutrality, turns to the United Nations, and requests the help of the great powers in defending the country's neutrality. I request Your Excellency to put on the agenda of the forthcoming General Assembly of the United Nations the question of Hungary's neutrality and the defence of this neutrality by the great powers.

AFTER THE RISING

> The new communist government of Hungary was led by a man called János Kádár. Under Kádár economic conditions in Hungary gradually improved.

> The supporters of the Rising were severely punished. Imre Nagy was executed in 1958.

> The Hungarian Uprising showed East Europeans that they could expect no help from the USA if they rose up against Soviet control. The US policy of 'containment' meant that the Americans would fight to stop the spread of communism but would not interfere if a country was already communist.

> There was a period of uneasy peace in Eastern Europe for the next 10 years. It was not until the mid-1960s that people in the satellite states once again challenged Soviet control. In 1968 the government of Czechoslovakia decided to develop a new form of communism that was much more liberal than Soviet communism.

> Communists around the world were dismayed by the way the Soviet Union used force against the Hungarian people. In Western Europe many communists were disillusioned. In China the leaders became more wary of Moscow.

> The invasion was a blow to the reputation of the United Nations. It did nothing to stop an act of aggression by one member state on another member state.

Czechoslovakia: 1968

Economic problems were a major cause of calls for reform in Czechoslovakia. The country had been economically successful before the Second World War. By the mid-1960s many people were very disappointed with the standard of living under Soviet-style communism. Czechoslovakia had also been a democracy before the war and people resented their lack of freedom of speech under the Soviet system. In 1966 there were student demonstrations and public criticism of the way the Soviet Union controlled the economy of Czechoslovakia. The student protesters called for greater democracy and free speech.

In January 1968 a new communist leader, Alexander Dubček, was appointed. He was determined to improve communism. His plans were described as 'socialism with a human face', and the early months of 1968 have become known as the 'Prague Spring'. Dubček began to introduce a number of reforms:

> the Soviet system of state planning would be altered to give more responsibility to farms and factories,

> trade unions would be given greater freedom,

> more foreign travel to the West would be allowed,

> censorship of the Press would be abolished so that people could say and write what they liked,

> criticism of the government would not be seen as a crime.

At the same time Dubček was still a communist. He did not want to introduce Western-style capitalism. Dubček knew what had happened in 1956. He tried to re-assure the Soviet leaders that his reforms were less radical than those called for during the Hungarian Uprising. He stated repeatedly that he wanted Czechoslovakia to remain a loyal member of the Warsaw Pact. He insisted that changes in Czechoslovakia were no threat to the security of the Soviet Union.

Brezhnev, the Soviet leader, did not accept these assurances from Dubček. He was afraid that once the communist system allowed free speech the country would become chaotic. Brezhnev felt that the Czechoslovak reforms were the first step towards the country leaving the communist bloc and becoming a Western-style country, allied to the USA. He was not prepared to allow this. Czechoslovakia was in an important strategic position. If it was allied to the USA, it would provide a corridor along which American forces could march from West Germany to the Soviet Ukraine. Brezhnev was also under pressure from hard-line communists in East Germany. They argued that if free speech was allowed in Czechoslovakia, people in all other Eastern bloc countries would demand the same rights. This would weaken the power of the communist parties throughout Eastern Europe.

SOURCE H

Dubček during the early days of the Prague Spring.

Help from the USA?

Brezhnev, the Soviet leader, began to plan an invasion of Czechoslovakia. By late July Soviet tanks and troops were massed on the Czechoslovak border. Brezhnev was encouraged by developments in the West. The American government was in crisis in the summer of 1968. There were race riots in the black districts of several cities. The war in Vietnam had gone disastrously wrong for the USA. Brezhnev calculated that there was no possibility of America taking any action to stop the invasion. The Vietnam crisis distracted attention from Czechoslovakia, just as in 1956 the Suez crisis reduced the impact of the invasion of Hungary.

SOURCE I

A letter of warning was sent by the Soviet leadership to the Czechoslovak Communist Party, 15 July 1968.

Developments in your country are causing deep anxiety among us. We are convinced that your country is being pushed off the road of socialism and that this puts in danger the interest of the whole socialist system.

We cannot agree to have hostile forces push your country away from the road of socialism. We cannot accept the risk of Czechoslovakia being cut off from the socialist community of countries. This is something more than your own concern. It is the common concern of all communist parties and states. It is the common concern of our countries, which have joined in the Warsaw Treaty to place an insurmountable barrier against the imperialist forces.

At great sacrifice the people of our countries achieved victory over Hitlerian fascism and won the opportunity to follow the path of socialism. The frontiers of the socialist world moved to the centre of Europe. And we shall never agree to these historic gains and the security of our peoples being placed in jeopardy. We shall never agree to imperialism making a breach in the socialist system of countries.

SOURCE J

Dubček's response to the Soviet threat made matters worse. He invited Tito, the independent communist leader of Yugoslavia, to Prague. Tito arrived on 9 August. To Brezhnev this seemed like a signal that Dubček was moving away from the Warsaw Pact and towards the same independent position taken by Yugoslavia. Dubček also entered into negotiations with the Romanian leader, Nicolae Ceaușescu. A pact of friendship between Czechoslovakia and Romania was signed. The Romanian leader also resented control from Moscow. The closer ties between these two countries seemed like an attempt to undermine Soviet control of the Warsaw Pact.

e Warsaw Pact forces invade

Soviet forces crossed the Czechoslovak frontier on 20 August 1968. They were joined by token forces from East Germany, Poland and Bulgaria. A day later the Warsaw Pact forces were in Prague, the capital of Czechoslovakia. Large-scale loss of life was avoided because the Czechoslovak government decided not to resist the invading army. People took to the streets to protest but there was none of the bloody street fighting that had taken place in Budapest in 1956. The Soviet troops took Dubček to Moscow and ordered him to abandon his reforms. He was finally removed from office in 1969. A pro-Soviet leader called Husák took his place. Soviet power was demonstrated in May 1970 when a Soviet–Czechoslovak treaty was signed. In this the Czechoslovaks were forced to thank the Soviets for the invasion.

Rioting in Prague as Soviet tanks take over the city. In contrast with Budapest, there was relatively little bloodshed in Prague.

THE AFTERMATH OF CZECHOSLOVAKIA 1968

After the invasion Brezhnev said that the Soviet Union was not prepared to let any communist country abandon communism. If a state did try to give up communism, the Soviet Union claimed the right to impose communism by force. This view became known as the Brezhnev Doctrine. The doctrine was finally abandoned in the 1980s.

The way the Soviet Union dealt with Czechoslovakia was less bloody than the treatment of Hungary after 1956. Nagy was executed. Dubček was thrown out of the communist party in 1970. He spent the 1970s and 1980s working as a forestry inspector. However, he kept his life and his freedom.

The government of China was unhappy at the invasion and it led to a further deterioration in relations between the two communist superpowers. The Chinese disliked the way the Soviet Union treated other communist countries. Afterwards, Mao encouraged Yugoslavia and Romania to remain independent of Moscow. There were border clashes between Soviet and Chinese troops in the months after the invasion.

The invasion disillusioned communists around the world. In Western Europe many communists stopped looking to Moscow for guidance. In the 1970s the powerful Italian and French communist parties called for a new style of communism that allowed free speech and free elections.

>> Activity

1 Explain in your own words why Brezhnev decided to invade Czechoslovakia in 1968.

2 Look back at the whole of this unit. What similarities and differences were there between the Hungarian Uprising and the invasion of Czechoslovakia? Think about the following aspects of each event:

> the causes of unrest,

> the aims of the people wanting change,

> the reasons why the Soviet Union found these changes unacceptable,

> the way the Soviet Union invaded,

> the treatment of the leadership after the invasion.

Building the Berlin Wall

In 1945 Berlin was divided into American, British, French and Soviet zones. Berlin itself was deep inside the Soviet zone of eastern Germany. This created a curious situation in Berlin. The American, British and French zones joined together to form a single area known as West Berlin. It became an island of Western capitalism in the middle of the communist sea of East Germany. In 1961 a wall was built to separate East and West Berlin. This became the most famous symbol of the Cold War.

Why was the Berlin Wall built?

BERLIN AND MOSCOW

The existence of West Berlin was very annoying to Soviet leaders in Moscow:

> It was much more prosperous than communist East Germany and was an advertisement for the economic success of Western Europe.

> Western governments used Berlin as a headquarters for their spying activities.

> German people could move freely from communist East Germany to West Berlin. Many decided to flee via West Berlin. Between 1949 and 1960, 3 million East Germans fled to the West through Berlin. These people were often young, talented and well-educated. The communist government could not afford to lose its future managers and leaders.

The crisis over Berlin was not simply about the problems the city posed for East Germany. It was part of the wider Cold War struggle between the USA and the USSR. In the early 1960s both countries had confident, aggressive leaders. The Soviet leader was Nikita Khrushchev and the American leader was John F. Kennedy. Each one was convinced that his side was right and each one was ready to threaten war to get what he wanted.

Khrushchev and the Soviet challenge

Nikita Khrushchev had emerged victorious from the power struggle that followed the death of Stalin in 1953. Khrushchev was confident that Soviet communism would eventually triumph over Western democracy and capitalism. He believed that the communist world was just about to overtake the West in wealth and scientific research. In October 1957 the Soviets launched the world's first ever satellite, called Sputnik. Khrushchev thought that this proved the strength of the communist world. Convinced of the increasing power of communism, Khrushchev decided to extend communist influence in Europe. He chose Berlin as the place for a trial of strength.

SOURCE A

In speeches made in 1958, Khrushchev expressed his view that Soviet communism was overtaking the West.

The launching of the Soviet sputniks first of all shows that a serious change has occurred in the balance of forces between socialist and capitalist countries, in favour of the socialist nations.

January, 1958

We are firmly convinced that the time is approaching when socialist countries will outstrip the most developed capitalist countries in the volume of industrial production.

October, 1958

Khrushchev calls for a neutral Berlin

The crisis that led to the building of the wall started in 1958 when Khrushchev called for the end of the four-power control of Berlin. He set a time limit of six months for the settlement of the future of Berlin. There was a vague threat of war if the matter was not resolved. His own plan was that Berlin should become a neutral free city and Western troops should withdraw. The Western powers were divided about how to react to Khrushchev. The West German leader, Konrad Adenauer, was strongly against any deal. By contrast, The US President, Eisenhower, was ready to negotiate over the future of Berlin. As the deadline approached Eisenhower made it clear that he did not want to risk a war over Berlin. Khrushchev dropped his ultimatum. At a summit meeting in September 1959 Eisenhower said that he was prepared to make concessions on the future of Berlin.

SOURCE C

Eisenhower's views at the 1959 summit:

We must remember that Berlin is an abnormal situation. It has come about through some mistakes of our leaders – Churchill and Roosevelt. There must be some way to develop some kind of free city which might somehow be part of West Germany. Perhaps the UN would become a party to guaranteeing the freedom, safety and security of the city. Berlin would have an unarmed status except for police forces. The time is coming, and perhaps soon, when we would simply have to get our forces out.

The U-2 spy plane incident

So far, Khrushchev had been very successful. Through threatening war he had divided the Western allies and won a promise of change from the US President, Eisenhower. Khrushchev and Eisenhower agreed to meet for further discussions about Berlin in May 1960.

This meeting did not take place. Just before it was due to start, an American U-2 spy plane was shot down over Soviet territory. The pilot, Gary Powers, was taken prisoner and put on trial. Khrushchev demanded an apology. Eisenhower refused to apologise. Khrushchev cancelled the summit meeting. As a result he missed his chance to do a deal over Berlin.

SOURCE B

An exhibition about Gary Powers and his U-2 spy plane, held in Moscow in 1960. The US government was extremely embarrassed by the U-2 incident.

A change of president

Eisenhower retired at the end of 1960. The new President was the young John F. Kennedy. In his election speeches Kennedy said that he was going to be tougher with the Soviets than Eisenhower.

SOURCE D

Extracts from John F. Kennedy's campaign speeches in 1960:

The enemy is the communist sytem itself – unceasing in its drive for world domination. This is a struggle for supremacy between two conflicting ideologies: freedom under God versus ruthless, godless tyranny.

We will mould our strength and become first again. Not first if. Not first but. Not first when. But first period. I want the world to wonder not what Mr Khrushchev is doing. I want them to wonder what the United States is doing.

The threat of war

Kennedy brought a new firm approach to the argument over Berlin. Kennedy and Khrushchev met in Vienna in June 1961. This was unfriendly and unsuccessful. Khrushchev demanded that Berlin should become neutral. He angrily talked about the danger of war if the USA refused to pull out of Berlin. Banging his hands on the conference table, Khrushchev said,'I want peace, but if you want war, that is your problem.' Kennedy ended the conference by saying, 'It's going to be a cold winter.'

SOURCE E

Kennedy and Khrushchev at the summit meeting in Vienna, 1961. At this meeting both sides threatened war.

Afterwards Khrushchev repeated his demands in public and insisted, as he had done with Eisenhower, that the USA must act within six months. At the same time he increased Soviet spending on defence by 30 per cent. Unlike Eisenhower, Kennedy was in no mood to do a deal. At the end of July Kennedy announced a complete rejection of the Soviet demands. He ordered a massive increase in the American armed services: the number of troops was increased by 15 per cent, spending on defence was increased by $3 billion and many new aircraft and warships were ordered. In public speeches both Kennedy and Khrushchev suggested that they were ready for war over Berlin:

SOURCE F

Kennedy made a television and radio speech to the American people on 25 July 1961.

I have heard it said that West Berlin is militarily untenable. Any dangerous spot is tenable if men – brave men – will make it so. We do not want to fight – but we have fought before. We cannot and will not permit the Communists to drive us out of Berlin, either gradually or by force. There is peace in Berlin today. The source of world trouble and tension is Moscow, not Berlin.

SOURCE G

In late July 1961 Khrushchev spoke to an American diplomat and threatened war:

If your troops try to force their way to Berlin, we will oppose you by force. War is bound to go thermonuclear, and though you and we may survive, all your European allies will be completely destroyed.

Behind the angry words it seems that neither side was really willing to start a nuclear war over the future of Berlin.

SOURCE H

On his way back from the Vienna summit Kennedy described his private thoughts.

It seems particularly stupid to risk killing a million Americans over an argument about access rights on an Autobahn or because the Germans want Germany reunified. If I'm going to threaten Russia with a nuclear war, it will have to be for much bigger and more important reasons than that.

Building the wall

While Khrushchev threatened nuclear war, he secretly planned a different solution to the Berlin crisis. The continued uncertainty over Berlin increased the number of East Germans who fled to West Berlin. Every day over a thousand East Germans entered the Western part of the city. In the early hours of 13 August 1961 barbed wire and barricades were erected all around West Berlin. When the people of West Berlin woke up their city was sealed off from East Germany. The barbed wire was later replaced by more substantial barriers; the Berlin Wall was created.

SOURCE I

An 18-year-old builder, Peter Fechter, shot dead behind the East Berlin side of the wall while trying to escape to the West.

WHO GAINED AND WHO LOST FROM THE BUILDING OF THE BERLIN WALL?

> The flow of refugees from East to West stopped almost completely. This allowed the communists to consolidate their control over East Germany.

> Enemies of communism could argue that communism was so awful that people had to be walled in to make sure that they did not run away from communism.

> Between 1948 and 1961 there was a real possibility that arguments about Berlin would lead to a Third World War. This possibility stopped with the building of the Berlin Wall.

> People in East Germany who did not support communism were now trapped. Those who tried to get over the wall were shot.

> The building of the wall was the beginning of a period of calm in Europe. On both sides people accepted that there was no immediate prospect of change and the level of tension went down.

>> Activity

Explain why the Berlin Wall was built. In your answer mention:

> how West Berlin came to exist,

> why West Berlin annoyed Soviet leaders,

> why Khrushchev was keen to confront the USA,

> the different reactions of Eisenhower and Kennedy to Soviet threats.

Solidarity

In 1980 a remarkable new development took place in Eastern Europe. Since the communist take-over in the 1940s Moscow had not allowed any real political opposition to communism in the countries of Eastern Europe. In Poland, in 1980, this changed. A powerful non-communist organisation called Solidarity challenged the government.

What part did Solidarity play in the decline of Soviet power?

The challenge of Poland

With a population of 35 million, Poland was, after the Soviet Union, the largest country in Eastern Europe and there were several reasons why the Soviets had problems controlling Poland:

1 Much of Poland had been ruled by Russia since the eighteenth century. Most Poles were proud of their nation and disliked Soviet communism.

2 The Second World War increased the Poles' hatred for Soviet Russia. Stalin had carved up their country with Hitler in 1939. In 1940 Stalin massacred thousands of Polish Army officers and buried them at Katyn. In 1944 the Soviet Red Army deliberately allowed the Warsaw Rising to fail, with huge loss of Polish life.

3 Most Poles were Catholics. The Catholic Church, which was too well-organised to be broken by the communists, encouraged Polish nationalism. In 1978 a leading Polish churchman became Pope John Paul II.

4 Ordinary Polish people had more power than in other communist countries. Polish farmers successfully held on to their own farms. Among Polish factory workers there was a strong tradition of using strikes against the government. In 1956 and 1970 strikes had forced the communist government to change both its leaders and its policies.

The birth of Solidarity

Polish living standards were poor in the 1970s. The communist government had large international debt. In July 1980 new price rises led to widespread unrest and strikes. Strikers were particularly active at the Lenin shipyards in the town of Gdansk (formerly Danzig). The workers at Gdansk were led by a remarkable man, an electrician called Lech Walesa. He was a brilliant speaker. In August the striking workers set up a new trade union called Solidarity. Unlike all other trade unions in communist states, Solidarity was not controlled by communists. Soon it had 9 million members and was demanding not only better conditions for workers, but also more political and religious freedom. Unrest spread throughout Poland. The communist leader, Gierek, was replaced in September as the communist party tried to find a way out of the crisis. In November, judges in the Polish Supreme Court sided with Solidarity and declared that the union was legal.

SOURCE A

Lech Walesa, the Solidarity leader, speaking at Gdansk, 1980.

Once Solidarity was formed and became a national force, the Polish communist leaders were in an impossible position:

> If they tried to destroy Solidarity they would be despised by the great majority of the Polish people.

> If they accepted the existence of a non-communist opposition force they risked provoking an armed invasion by the USSR.

Send in the tanks?

In December 1980 and March 1981 the Soviet leaders considered sending troops into Poland to impose Soviet power, just as they had done in Hungary in 1956 and Czechoslovakia in 1968. They decided against immediate armed intervention but urged the Polish communists to destroy Solidarity before it got out of control. A new Polish Prime Minister was appointed called Wojciech Jaruzelski. He was a communist and an army general. The Soviet leaders made it clear to him that he must control Solidarity or expect a Soviet invasion.

SOURCE C

Speaking in 1995, Jaruzelski described the pressures that were put on him in 1981.

At first the Soviets gave us an ultimatum: either bring the situation under control or we will cut off supplies of oil, gas and other raw materials. I was summoned three times to the Soviet Union. On the last occasion, in September 1981, I was shown army manoeuvres all along the Polish border. The Soviet army leader, Marshal Ustinov, informed me that what was happening in Poland was intolerable. We had to convince our allies that we would not undermine the Warsaw Pact or allow the state to be de-stabilised. The introduction of martial law allowed us to avoid military intervention.

SOURCE B

General Jaruzelski. The communist leader knew that if he did not control Solidarity, Soviet tanks could invade Poland.

Martial law

Jaruzelski tried to negotiate with Solidarity but the talks were not successful. In December 1981 he took the advice from Moscow and declared a state of martial law in Poland. This meant that the army had emergency powers. The leaders of Solidarity and thousands of its supporters were arrested and held without trial. Meetings and demonstrations were forbidden. Many supporters of Solidarity lost their jobs. In October 1982 the government tried to replace Soldarity with new communist unions.

Jaruzelski's attempt to destroy Solidarity did not work. Walesa was imprisoned but this made him seem even more of a hero. The movement survived underground. No one took the new unions seriously. Communist party members left the party in huge numbers. Almost a year after the declaration of martial law, in November 1982, Walesa was released from prison.

SOURCE E

A British newspaper later summed up the impact of martial law on Walesa while in prison:

Walesa waited, his message to the government the same, 'You will have to talk to us again. Without the public consent, which only Solidarity can deliver, your economic reforms can never succeed.' The claim was the simple truth.

He emerged from prison to a surprising discovery – Poland was not a political wasteland. In addition to the Solidarity underground network there were new groupings producing an extraordinary range of newspapers, journals and books. Far from being snuffed out, the opposition to Communist rule had been broadened and strengthened.

The *Observer*, 'Tearing down the Curtain', 1990

SOURCE D

In 1983 Walesa was awarded a Nobel Prize for his work for Solidarity. In the same year the Pope visited Poland and was greeted with great enthusiasm. He was another symbol of hope for Polish opponents of communism. In 1984, Polish people were outraged to learn that Father Jerzy Popielusko, a priest who supported the union, had been beaten to death by secret police. The continuing support for Solidarity was shown when a quarter of a million people attended his funeral.

Huge enthusiastic crowds turned out to greet Pope John Paul II during his visit to Poland in 1983.

The impact of Gorbachev

In 1985 the political mood in Poland began to change because of the rise to power of Gorbachev in the USSR. By calling for greater freedom in the Soviet Union Gorbachev undermined old-style communism in Eastern Europe. The threat of Russian tanks also began to disappear.

Jaruzelski introduced reforms similar to those being tried in the USSR under Gorbachev. Jaruzelski held a referendum in November 1987 asking for backing for his economic reforms. He failed to win enough votes which was a great blow to his authority. In 1988 Walesa and the still illegal Solidarity organised a nationwide series of strikes against price rises. Walesa called for talks with the government and finally Jaruzelski agreed. As a result of these talks Solidarity was once again legalised and elections were organised for June 1989.

Solidarity triumphs in elections

For the first time since the 1940s free elections were being held in Eastern Europe but the freedom was limited. They were organised so that 65 per cent of seats in the main chamber of the Polish Parliament were reserved for communists. Nevertheless, the elections were a disaster for the communists. So few people voted for them that they looked ridiculous. Almost all leading communists failed to get elected. The Polish people voted massively for Solidarity. In the Polish Senate, the second chamber of the Polish parliament, there were no restrictions and Solidarity won 99 out of 100 seats. Weeks of chaos followed as the discredited communists tried and failed to form a government. Eventually, Jaruzelski agreed that Solidarity could help to form a government. In August, Tadeuz Mazowiecki, a leading member of Solidarity, became the Prime Minister of a coalition government that included both communist and Solidarity ministers. In less than a year Solidarity had gone from being illegal to being the leading part of the government. The remaining communist ministers soon resigned and the Solidarity take-over was complete.

SOURCE F

Bronislaw Geremek was a leading Solidarity activist. He reacted emotionally when in August 1989 Solidarity helped to form a government:

For the first time in 45 years, a Polish government is to be formed, on Polish soil, by non-Communist forces. The monopoly of the Party which ruled Poland against the will of the people has been broken.

>> Activity

1 Explain in your own words why the Soviet Union had always found it difficult to control Poland.

2 Why were the leaders of the Soviet Union worried when Solidarity was set up in 1980–81?

3 How successful was the introduction of martial law?

4 How did Solidarity take power in 1989?

SOURCE G

A Solidarity demonstration in 1989. In that year Solidarity triumphed in elections.

The arms race

Throughout the period of the Cold War, the two sides competed to outdo each other with the quantity and quality of their weapons and armed forces. For most of the time the Americans had the upper hand but they were constantly fearful of being overtaken by the Soviet Union.

THE GROWTH OF THE NUCLEAR ARSENALS

1945   Only the Americans had atomic bombs

1949   The USSR exploded its first atomic bomb in August

1952   The Americans exploded the first more powerful hydrogen bomb in November

1953   In August the Soviet government exploded a hydrogen bomb

1957   The Soviets developed the world's first intercontinental ballistic missile (ICBM)

1958   In January the Americans tested their first ICBM

1959   An American submarine armed with nuclear Polaris missiles was launched in June

---

Conventional forces grow

The Americans were also worried by the sheer number of soldiers and so-called 'conventional' (non-nuclear) weapons possessed by the Soviet Union. In 1950 North Korean forces invaded South Korea and the Americans attacked in support of the non-communist South Koreans. The Korean War led to a huge increase in American spending on soldiers and weapons. US ground forces tripled in numbers between 1950 and 1953. US spending on defence soared from $11 billion in 1948 to $50 billion in 1953.

The missile gap?

In the late 1950s many Americans believed that the Soviet Union had more ICBMs than the US, which they called the 'missile gap'. The missile gap did not exist but between 1960 and 1962, under President Kennedy, US defence expenditure rose from $45 billion to $52 billion and a range of new battlefield nuclear weapons were developed that could be used against the Soviet tank armies. In 1957 the Soviets launched a sputnik, the first ever satellite, and in April 1961 the Soviet cosmonaut, Yuri Gagarin, became the first man in space. This event, like the launch of sputnik, increased American fears, but both governments secretly knew that the Americans were still the more powerful nuclear force. The US authorities had accurate information about Soviet military strength. From 1957 their U-2 spy planes, which could take photographs from 70,000 feet, indicated that the Soviets had only a limited number of ICBMs and that the USA continued to have a massive superiority in nuclear weapons.

The Soviets catch up

The Cuban missile crisis of October 1962 almost led to nuclear war between the two superpowers. Afterwards there was a desire on both sides to avoid a similar crisis. In August 1963 the Soviets, Americans and British agreed that they would not carry out further nuclear tests in the air or underwater. However, after Khrushchev fell from power in 1964, his successor, Leonid Brezhnev, increased Soviet spending on weapons. The USA was bogged down in the Vietnam War, and by 1971 the Soviets had finally caught up with the Americans in terms of the number of nuclear missiles. This was achieved at great cost – as much as a quarter of the Soviet national income was spent on defence.

The SALT Agreements

After 1971 there was a period of co-operation, or 'détente'. The Soviet leaders were alarmed at the cost of the arms race and the Americans wanted better relations with the communist world as they tried to end the Vietnam War. In 1972 the two superpowers finally agreed to limit the use of ICBMs when they signed the SALT 1 (Strategic Arms Limitation Talks) Agreement. Although this agreement was a great breakthrough, many nuclear weapons were not covered by the treaty. In the 1979 SALT 2 talks, agreement was reached covering a wider range of nuclear weapons but this agreement never came into force because, after the Soviet invasion of Afghanistan in 1979, the Americans refused to ratify the treaty.

Star Wars

In November 1980 Ronald Reagan was elected as US President. He loathed communism and in the first four years of his presidency he increased spending on arms by over 40 per cent. These years are sometimes called the new, or second, Cold War. Both sides deployed so-called intermediate nuclear missiles – the Soviet SS-20s and the NATO Pershing and Cruise Missiles. The US missiles were more sophisticated than the Soviet equivalents – they could avoid radar and could be launched from almost anywhere. Reagan's Strategic Defence Initiative, known as SDI or Star Wars, started in 1983. Reagan announced that American scientists were developing laser weapons to shoot down Soviet missiles from space.

The end of the arms race

By the mid 1980s, with their economy in trouble, the Soviet government found it difficult to compete with the West. A new Soviet leader – Mikhail Gorbachev – came to power in 1985. He was committed to the idea of peace with the non-communist world. The arrival of Gorbachev almost immediately transformed superpower relations and led to the Intermediate Nuclear Weapons Treaty in 1987. This involved substantial disarmament – all intermediate nuclear missiles were to be removed from Europe within three years. In December 1988 Gorbachev addressed the United Nations General Assembly in New York and announced that the Soviet Union no longer wished to build up unnecessary stockpiles of arms. The personnel of the Soviet army was immediately reduced by half a million people; 50,000 men and 5,000 tanks were withdrawn from Eastern Europe. Gorbachev's speech signalled the end of the arms race. The removal of the Soviet threat contributed to the collapse of communism in Eastern Europe in 1989. With the disintegration of the Soviet Union in 1991 the USA stood unchallenged as the world's most powerful military state.

THE ARMS RACE IN 1963

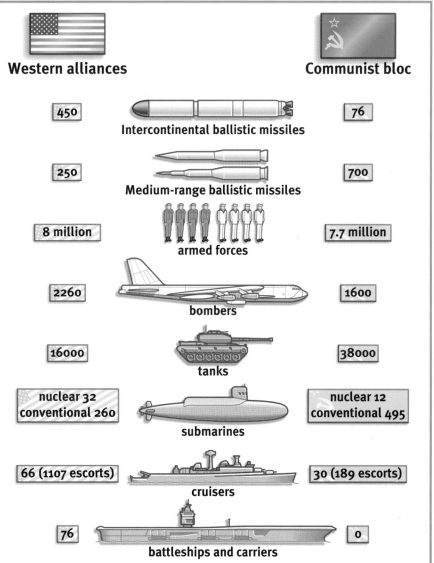

The diagram shows the number of arms each of the superpowers had in early 1963, just after the Cuban missile crisis. The nuclear balance was 5 to 1 in favour of the USA. By 1971 the Soviets had as many nuclear weapons as the Americans, but the enormous cost of this achievement had caused great damage to the Soviet economy.

© Based on Bartholomew mapping 1993   MM–0097–35

Discussion points

> How did the technology of warfare change in the 1950s?

> What happened during the period of détente in the 1970s?

> Why was détente replaced by a second Cold War in the early 1980s?

> How did the arms race come to an end?

> Which superpower do you think was more successful in the arms race?

Gorbachev and the fall of the Soviet Empire

Between 1985 to 1991 Mikhail Gorbachev was the leader of the USSR. In 1989 Soviet control of Eastern Europe collapsed. In 1991 the Soviet Union fell apart.

Was Gorbachev responsible for the collapse of communism in Europe?

Focus

Look at the following information about the Soviet Union and Eastern Europe before Gorbachev came to power. What were the long-term causes for the collapse of communism?

The standard of living

In the early 1960s, communists had been convinced that communism was better than capitalism and that the communist states would soon produce more goods than in the USA and Western Europe. By the 1980s it was clear that communism had failed to deliver high living standards. Most people in the Soviet Union and Eastern Europe were much poorer than the people of Western Europe. Some basic goods, such as sugar, were rationed. The gap between communist and capitalist economies was growing all the time. The Soviet Union and its allies were not able to compete with the West in the new industries of the 1980s – computers and telecommunications.

By the 1980s Soviet farming had failed. The Soviet Union had rich land at its disposal but it could not produce enough food to feed its people. Many people worked on the land but they were very inefficient. In the 1980s farming employed over 20 per cent of the workforce, compared with 3 per cent in the USA. On average each American farmer produced seven times more food than each Soviet farmer. As a result the USSR had to import millions of tons of grain, much of it from the USA.

SOURCE A

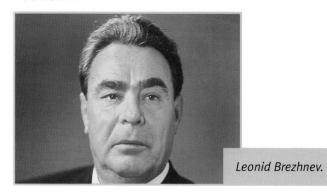

Leonid Brezhnev.

Corruption and the decline of communism

The founders of communism promised a new kind of state based on fairness and equality. Under the leadership of Brezhnev, Soviet communism moved a long way from these ideals and became more corrupt. As a result ordinary people had less respect for communism. It was widely known that the family of Brezhnev was corrupt. Leading communists had luxurious country houses or 'dachas' built for themselves. According to one joke that circulated in the Soviet Union at the time, Brezhnev showed his own mother round a new luxury house that he had just had built; his mother commented 'It's wonderful, Leonid. But what happens if the communists come back to power?'

A second Cold War

With the communist economies in trouble, the cost of the Cold War became more and more unbearable. The price of weapons was constantly increasing. By the 1980s a single bomber cost the same as 200 bombers built during the Second World War. America and its allies could afford these higher costs because their economies were doing well. The Soviet Union could only keep up with the USA by diverting a huge proportion of its national income to defence. People suffered even lower living standards as tanks were built instead of cars and televisions.

The cost of the Cold War began to increase when the US President, Ronald Reagan, came to power in 1981. He rejected the idea of detente and encouraged a policy of confrontation with the Soviets. He took the view that communism was wicked and needed to be approached with great firmness. Reagan increased military spending and challenged the USSR to join a new arms race.

The early 1980s have been called the 'Second Cold War' because there was heightened tension between the USA and the Soviet Union. The competition between the superpowers was symbolised by Reagan's 'Star Wars' project (officially known as SDI: the Strategic Defence Initiative). This project involved research into ways of giving America nuclear superiority by destroying Soviet missiles in space.

War in Afghanistan

Brezhnev made a big mistake in December 1979. Soviet troops invaded Afghanistan to support its communist government. The invasion was widely criticised and lost the USSR many friends. It led to a widespread boycott of the Olympic Games that were held in Moscow. Afghanistan was a Muslim country and the USSR was criticised by much of the Islamic world. The Afghan rebels received help from the USA and the invasion encouraged Reagan to take a tough anti-Soviet stance when he became president in 1980.

The Soviet military action was a failure. The official Afghan army was not strong enough to win alone and once the Soviet forces had become involved it became very difficult to withdraw. With Soviet help the Afghan government controlled Kabul, the capital, and other large towns, but the rebels controlled much of the countryside. More and more Soviet troops were needed to prop up an unpopular government. In the early 1980s there were about 125,000 Soviet troops in the country.

The situation of the Soviets in Afghanistan was similar to that of the Americans in Vietnam a decade earlier. The 10-year war led to the death of about 15,000 Soviet troops. It also damaged the Soviet economy: one estimate is that the war cost the USSR about $8 billion dollars a year. The last Soviet troops finally left Afghanistan in February 1989.

SOURCE B

Soviet troops fighting anti-communist forces in Afghanistan. The war in Afghanistan damaged the international reputation of the Soviet Union.

Andropov and Gorbachev

The ideas of Gorbachev were not completely original. By 1980 there were many younger, idealistic communists who were disgusted by corruption and wanted to reform the system. Several reformers gathered around the head of the KGB, Yuri Andropov. Gorbachev was one of this group. Brezhnev died in 1982 and Andropov became the new Soviet leader. Within a few months he became desperately ill and he died in February 1984. Although he was not in power long, Andropov introduced some policies that were later developed by Gorbachev:

> He called for an end to the arms race, and offered to reduce the Soviet stockpile of weapons in return for American reductions.

> He attacked corruption at home.

Andropov made a number of offers to Reagan. One of these was revolutionary – this was a plan to abandon the Brezhnev Doctrine and to promise never again to invade other Warsaw Pact countries. Reagan did not take this offer seriously and it came to nothing. Although Andropov had many original ideas he did little to provide more freedom for the people of the Soviet Union. As the KGB Chairman from 1967–82 he had played a key role in the persecution of dissidents, nationalists and different religious groups. After the death of Andropov, the new leader of the Soviet Union was Konstantin Chernenko. He had little interest in reform. Like Andropov, Chernenko did not live long enough to have much impact. He died in 1985 and his replacement as General Secretary was the reformer Mikhail Gorbachev. He introduced policies of 'glasnost' or 'openness' and 'perestroika' or 'economic restructuring'.

One critical difference between Gorbachev and Andropov was in the way glasnost gave new freedom to the people of the Soviet Union. This was a radical change. Control of ideas had always been a central part of the Soviet system. Under glasnost, people were told an increasing amount about the atrocities committed by the government when Stalin had been in power. Thousands of political prisoners were released. The leading dissident Andrei Sakharov was released in 1986.

THE GORBACHEV AGENDA

> The economy was failing. The communist system needed to be reformed but not replaced. This would be done by a process called 'perestroika' or 'restructuring'.

> Perestroika would require a new honesty on the part of people in the Soviet Union. Free speech should be allowed. There should be a new spirit of 'glasnost' or 'openness'. There should be an end to the persecution of the dissidents.

> Corruption must be stamped out.

> A key cause of the economic problems was the amount of money being spent on defence. To reduce this the Soviet Union should:

pull out of Afghanistan

negotiate arms reductions with the USA

stop interfering in the affairs of other communist countries.

Another distinctive feature of the Gorbachev leadership was the energy and imagination with which he pursued the idea of disarmament with the US president, Reagan. Unlike Andropov he was able to persuade Reagan that he genuinely wanted an end to the Cold War. The two men met, face-to-face, at a series of summit meetings. The main focus for these discussions was arms control. The result was a major disarmament treaty in 1987. Both the USA and the Soviet Union agreed to remove medium-range nuclear missiles from Europe within three years.

Withdrawal from Afghanistan

As soon as he was in office, Gorbachev began to explore ways of ending the war in Afghanistan without destroying the communist government in that country. In February 1988 he announced publicly that the Soviet army was going to pull out of Afghanistan. The withdrawal began in May 1988. By February 1989 the last Soviet troops had left.

Failure at home

Gorbachev had many triumphs in foreign policy but he was less successful at home. By encouraging free speech, Gorbachev simply brought problems out into the open. He wanted to make the Soviet system of centrally planned production more efficient. This did not happen. The levels of corruption and inefficiency in the economy were too great. The managers of the Soviet economy saw the reforms as a threat to their jobs and they blocked the changes.

>> Activity

1 What similarities and differences were there between the policies of Andropov and those of Gorbachev?

2 What can you learn from Sources C and D about the motives of Gorbachev?

SOURCE C

Gorbachev 1987:

I want to put an end to all the rumours in the West, and point out once again that all our reforms are socialist. We are looking within socialism, rather than outside it, for the answers to all the questions that arise. Those who hope that we shall move away from the socialist path will be greatly disappointed.

SOURCE D

In 1992, after he had lost power, Gorbachev tried to make sense of his years in control:

I knew that an immense task of transformation awaited me. Engaged in the exhausting arms race, the country, it was evident, was at the end of its strength. Economic mechanisms were functioning more and more poorly. Production figures were slumping. Scientific and technical developments were cancelled out by an economy totally in the hands of the bureaucracy. The people's standard of living was clearly declining. Corruption was gaining ground. We wanted to reform by launching a democratic process. It was similar to earlier reform attempts.

SOURCE E

Gorbachev and Reagan, 1987. The two men established a warm personal relationship and agreed to substantial disarmament.

The end of the Brezhnev Doctrine

Another foreign policy breakthrough came in December 1988, when Gorbachev spoke at the United Nations. He announced huge cuts in the Soviet armed forces. Gorbachev also made it clear that the Brezhnev Doctrine was now abandoned: the countries of Eastern Europe could do what they liked. There would be no more Soviet tanks rolling into Prague or Budapest.

SOURCE F

*Gorbachev, speaking to the United Nations on
7 December 1988:*

Force or the threat of force neither can nor should be instruments of foreign policy. The principle of the freedom of choice is mandatory. Refusal to recognise this principle will have serious consequences for world peace. To deny a nation the choice, regardless of any excuse, is to upset the unstable balance that has been achieved. Freedom of choice is a universal principle. It knows no exception.

SOURCE G

1989: year of revolution

When it became clear that the Soviet Union was no longer ready to use force to control its Empire, there was rapid change. In May 1989 the Hungarian government opened the frontier with Austria; there was now a gap in the Iron Curtain. In June free elections were held in Poland. Solidarity won and in August led a new non-communist government. Gorbachev expressed support for a peaceful hand-over of power. The rolling back of communism in Eastern Europe had begun. Many young East Germans made their way to Hungary and passed though Austria into West Germany. This made a nonsense of the Berlin Wall.

In October 1989 Gorbachev visited East Germany for the celebration of the fortieth anniversary of the state. Behind the scenes Gorbachev explained to East German leaders that he had no intention of using Russian force to stop reform. A month later, on 10 November, the Berlin Wall was torn down. The most famous symbol of the Cold War had been destroyed. On 17 November a series of massive anti-communist demonstrations took place in Czechoslovakia. By early December the Czechoslovak communist government had collapsed. On 21 December a revolution began in Romania. The Romanian dictator, Ceauşescu, was executed on Christmas Day. Throughout Eastern Europe there was no popular support for communism and, without the threat of Soviet tanks, communism fell apart. In 1990 the two halves of Germany were re-united and a single pro-Western state was established.

The collapse of European communism was symbolised by the fall of the Berlin Wall, November 1989.

The last days of the USSR

After 1989 Gorbachev was in a difficult position. His plan to reform communism had failed. Communism had been rejected by Eastern Europe and different nationalities demanded independence from the Soviet Union. The call for independence was strongest in the Baltic republics of Latvia, Lithuania and Estonia. In Russia itself, the heart of the USSR, many people demanded an end to communism. On 4 February 1990, 250,000 people demonstrated in Moscow against communism.

With his plans in ruins Gorbachev responded by drawing back from reform and trying to make an alliance with old style, hard-line communists. On May Day 1990, demonstrators humiliated Gorbachev by shouting at him in public during the traditional communist march.

The rise of Yeltsin

Boris Yeltsin became the leader of the reformists. He had been a communist boss in the city of Moscow until he was dismissed in 1987 by Gorbachev because of his radical views. In May 1990 Yeltsin was elected President of Russia. The USSR was divided into separate republics and Russia was the largest of them. A month later Yeltsin left the communist party and joined forces with those who wanted to destroy Soviet communism. Gorbachev was losing control of events.

In the autumn of 1990 Gorbachev tried to stop the disintegration of the USSR by using force against nationalists in the Baltic republics. At the same time Gorbachev appointed more old-style communists to key positions of government. This new hard line from Gorbachev was not a success. He began to lose many of his long-standing friends and supporters. In December 1990 the Soviet Foreign Minister, Eduard Shevardnadze, resigned and complained of a move towards dictatorship. This was a great blow – Shevardnadze had been one of Gorbachev's allies for many years.

The fall of Gorbachev

The struggle for control of the USSR came to a head in 1991. Yeltsin attacked the power of the communist party in the daily life of Russian people. He banned the party from operating at all places of work. The Russian Parliament that Yeltsin controlled became more powerful and challenged the central government of Gorbachev. Gorbachev did not know which way to turn. In August 1991 a group of hard-line communists tried to seize power. They arrested Gorbachev and declared a state of emergency. The coup was opposed by Boris Yeltsin and it soon collapsed. After the coup, the authority of Gorbachev was damaged. In December 1991 the individual Soviet republics became independent and Gorbachev resigned as Soviet leader. The Soviet state, born in the 1917 revolution, no longer existed.

SOURCE H

Boris Yeltsin at the time of the 1991 coup. Yeltsin took power in Russia as the Soviet Union fell apart.

>> ## Activity

Explain the part that Gorbachev played in the collapse of communism in Eastern Europe and the Soviet Union. In your answer discuss:

a the long-term causes of the crisis for communism,

b the personal contribution of Gorbachev.

The Soviet Empire 1948–91

The split with Tito

The Yugoslav communist leader, Tito, liberated Yugoslavia from German control without help from Moscow. He argued with Stalin and refused to take orders from Moscow. In 1948 Yugoslavia was expelled from Cominform, the international grouping of communist parties. The Soviet Union imposed a trade ban on Yugoslavia but they survived due to support from the USA. Stalin dealt ruthlessly with other East European countries between 1949 and 1953. He was worried that they might try to copy Tito. Leading communists with independent ideas were imprisoned or executed.

TURMOIL IN THE COMMUNIST WORLD AFTER STALIN

> After Stalin's death in 1953 people in Eastern Europe hoped for more freedom from Soviet control.

> The new Soviet leader, Khrushchev, established friendly relations with Yugoslavia in 1955. Hungarians hoped to copy Yugoslav independence.

> In 1956 unrest in Poland led to reforms and concessions by the communist government. This encouraged Hungarians to demand reforms.

The Hungarian Uprising

In October 1956 unrest in Hungary led to the appointment of a new Prime Minister, the communist reformer, Imre Nagy. People demanded that Hungary should leave the Warsaw Pact and become neutral. Nagy agreed but in November 1956 Soviet troops invaded Hungary and imposed a new pro-Soviet government. There was fierce street fighting in which thousands of people were killed. Nagy was arrested and later executed. The USA did nothing to help the Hungarians: people in the West were preoccupied with the Suez crisis.

The Prague Spring

Economic problems caused unrest in Czechoslovakia in 1967. A new communist leader, Dubček, took power in January 1968. He introduced democratic reforms while remaining communist. In August 1968 Soviet troops invaded Czechoslovakia to end the reforms. Dubček lost his job in 1969 and a pro-Soviet government was put in place. Afterwards the Soviet leader, Brezhnev, announced the 'Brezhnev Doctrine': the Soviet Union would use force to keep communists in power in any country.

1956 AND 1968 COMPARED

> In both cases the Soviet Union used force to end reforms in East European countries. New pro-Soviet governments were imposed.

> The Hungarian government wanted to break with the Soviet Union, leave the Warsaw Pact and become neutral. The Czechoslovak government wanted much more democracy at home but promised to stay in the Warsaw Pact.

> In both cases the USA did nothing to help. The West was preoccupied with Suez in 1956 and Vietnam in 1968.

> The Hungarians fought against the Soviet invasion – thousands were killed. The Czechoslovak people offered non-violent resistance. The Hungarian leader, Nagy, was executed; the Czechoslovak leader, Dubček, lost his job but remained alive and free.

The Berlin Wall

Between 1958 and 1961 there was a dispute between the Soviet Union and the USA over Berlin. The Soviet leader, Khrushchev, said that Western forces should leave the city and that it should become neutral. The US president, Eisenhower, was prepared to compromise but he was replaced in 1961 by President Kennedy. Kennedy refused to compromise and both leaders publicly threatened war over Berlin. In 1961 the crisis was resolved, and the threat of immediate war disappeared, when a wall was built around West Berlin to stop East Germans fleeing the communist state.

Poland and the rise of Solidarity

Shipyard workers in Gdansk went on strike in 1980 in protest against rising prices. They were led by Lech Walesa and formed a new non-communist trade union called Solidarity. Millions of workers joined Solidarity. The Soviet government considered invading Poland in order to crush the union. To avoid this the Polish communist leader, Jaruzelski, banned Solidarity in December 1981. He declared martial law and imprisoned Solidarity leaders without trial but failed to destroy the union. Solidarity did well in elections in 1989 and formed a non-communist government.

SOVIET COMMUNISM IN DECLINE

The Soviet Union was in crisis by the early 1980s:

> The economy had failed to match the economies of America and Western Europe.

> The arms race further reduced living standards.

> There was widespread corruption.

> The Soviet Union was fighting a disastrous war in Afghanistan.

The second Cold War

After the Vietnam War the USA pursued a policy of detente with the Soviet Union. This involved peaceful co-existence and some arms reductions. Ronald Reagan became president of the USA in 1981 and he ended détente and began a new arms race with the USSR.

Gorbachev

Mikhail Gorbachev, a reformist communist, took control in the Soviet Union in 1985. He wanted to improve the Soviet Union by 'perestroika' – 'restructuring' or reforming the economy – and 'glasnost' – greater 'openness' and freedom of speech. His reforms undermined the position of old-style pro-Soviet leaders in other countries. He renounced the 'Brezhnev Doctrine' of interference in other countries.

The whole of communist Europe was swept with revolution in 1989. One by one, the communist authorities were overthrown. The Soviet Union led by Gorbachev did nothing to stop this process. The Berlin Wall was torn down in November 1989. In 1991 the Soviet Union fell apart. After a failed communist coup in August, the republics that made up the USSR declared their independence. Gorbachev resigned. Russia became a separate state ruled over by Boris Yeltsin.

Crowds outside the Reichstag celebrate the reunification of Germany, 3 October 1990.

Index